VICTORIA OCAMPO

Writer, Feminist, Woman of the World

TRANSLATED AND EDITED BY

Patricia Owen Steiner

UNIVERSITY OF NEW MEXICO PRESS

ALBUQUERQUE

© 1999 by the University of New Mexico Press
All rights reserved.
First edition

Library of Congress
Cataloging-in-Publication Data

Ocampo, Victoria, 1890–1979
[Selections. English. 1999]
Victoria Ocampo:
writer, feminist, woman of the world
translated by Patricia Owen Steiner
p.cm
ISBN 0-8263-2003-1 (cloth)
ISBN 0-8263-2994-x (pbk)
1. Ocampo, Victoria, 1890–1979
I. Steiner, Patricia Owen
II.Title.
PQ7797.O295A613 1999
868—dc21 98-40789
CIP
Designed by Sue Niewiarowski

CONTENTS

PREFACE

I first met Victoria Ocampo in 1979 on the obituary page of the *New York Times*.[1] Giving her prominent space, top and center, it described her as an "Argentine writer, publisher of the international literary magazine *Sur* and an exponent of cultural bridges between intellectuals in the Americas and Europe." It commented on her "aloof, aristocratic manner and dark beauty" and proclaimed that she was "a figure of admiration and condemnation among leading intellectual figures of her time, as much for being a woman of strong intellectual independence as for her literary work." It went on to note that she came from a wealthy family in Buenos Aires, chose to write mostly in French, was accustomed to extravagant impulses, and had published the works of such luminaries as T. S. Eliot, Marcel Proust, Albert Camus, Jorge Luis Borges, Langston Hughes, and Richard Wright. What especially caught my attention were two items: first, in 1967 Ocampo had been awarded an honorary degree by Harvard University, only the tenth woman to be so honored in its 330 years, and, second, she had been a friend and correspondent of Virginia Woolf. Here was a woman about whom I wanted to know more.

I soon learned that Victoria Ocampo had left behind a long and significant literary trail: ten volumes of essays (her *Testimonios*), several books of nonfiction, and a children's fable. I read through a great many of her essays, essays with such diverse titles as "The Grapes of Wrath," "Impressions of Nuremberg," "Gandhi," and "A Page on Dante." The essays that most interested me had titles such as "Virginia Woolf, Orlando and Co.," "Emily Brontë (terra incognita)," "Woman and Her Expression," and "Answer to an Epilogue by Ortega y Gasset." I began to see a facet of Victoria Ocampo that her obituary never mentioned: a not so latent feminist.

Five years later I returned from a trip to Buenos Aires with the six volumes of Victoria Ocampo's autobiography, published posthumously between 1979 and 1984. It was captivating, intimate; Ocampo now emerged, not just as a writer, a publisher, a builder of intellectual bridges, but as a woman of flesh and very warm blood. Ocampo's autobiography offers a new and extremely personal look at her early life, but it does more than make an impressive addition to the literature on Ocampo. It records in vibrant detail what it was like to grow up female in Argentina in the early part of the twentieth century—and, beyond that, what it feels like to be a young, ambitious, sensitive girl rebelling against a society with rigid preconceptions about the role of women. Beatriz Sarlo called Ocampo's autobiography "perhaps the most detailed history of a woman [in Argentina] that you could find in this whole period."[2] Articulating the significant contribution of Ocampo's autobiography, Doris Meyer characterized it in this way: "As the document of an era in Latin American cultural history, and particularly women's history, [it] is invaluable; as a work of autobiographical literature, it is a unique example of female discourse and definition."[3]

I have now been reading and translating and thinking about Ocampo for almost twenty years. Because I consider her feminism to be a defining characteristic and one of her most important contributions, I have chosen to highlight Ocampo's essays on women, approaching them through her autobiography and trying to understand the young woman who developed into the writer who produced them.

Part I, with its long excerpts from her autobiography, tells about the early years that are crucial to comprehending the essayist and feminist who was struggling to emerge. We see her as a spirited child, a rebellious adolescent; we follow her through a disastrous marriage, a scandalous affair, and relations with an array of famous men; finally we see her as a writer with influential connections on three continents. Ocampo's voice is personal and surprisingly candid. Her fears and weaknesses are exposed as well as the tender, passionate, tempestuous facets of her nature. Part II traces her subsequent development, as a person, as a feminist, and as an essayist of strong convictions. Part III presents an overview of her feminist essays as well as excerpts from translations of her essays on women. (The translations, unless otherwise noted, are my own.)

People write their autobiographies for a variety of reasons, most of them self-serving, and Victoria Ocampo was no exception. When, in her sixties, she settled down to write the story of her first forty years, she acknowledged that she wrote it to get a head start on her biographers, to set the record straight. There is surely, too, the intent to convince future readers of the importance of her influence and her ideas. Mostly, though, she wrote her autobiography as an exercise in self-discovery, in a conscious effort to make sense of her life as she began to entertain premonitions of her own mortality.

I believe that another motive for the autobiography was to show that a woman can be influential in her own right, not merely as a companion—or muse—for an important man. Ocampo begins her autobiography with a chapter on her ancestors. It doesn't take long to realize that, from Ocampo's and society's point of view, the only prestigious people in her family were men. Ocampo is obviously proud of these men—men of action, early conquistadores, settlers, diplomats, political leaders. The women in her family took secondary roles as mothers, wives, and daughters to this long line of prominent males.

What is clear is that there were no strong female models here for a young girl starting off to make her mark in life. Victoria knew these women only through their portraits or from the occasional family anecdote. She mentions no provocative diaries, no inspiring letters, no outstanding accomplishments. Their lives and their voices, however meaningful they may have been, are sadly lost. Among the women she knew in her immediate family, none stand out as persons of exceptional achievement. I suspect that it was from just such obscurity that Ocampo hoped to save herself.

Since most of Ocampo's writing was published either in her own journal or by her own publishing house, it seems likely that her works did not receive as much critical editing as might have been merited. For while her works have many lyrical passages, some memorable scenes of great intensity, and original approaches to feminist argument, they sometimes have a rambling, repetitious quality, a tendency to digress, even a slipping into sentimental excess. I have tried to edit her work in such a way as to avoid what seem to me to be her stylistic shortcomings and yet give the reader the best of Ocampo's autobiography and writing on women. Her most compelling writing, I believe, was about herself and about women and problems that still concern women today and that largely remain unsolved. Ocampo's voice from decades ago speaks cogently to the modern reader.

As the editor of *Sur* and a writer, Victoria Ocampo was a major figure in twentieth-century Latin American letters. But she was much more than that. She was also an iconoclast in a patriarchal society, a woman who chose not to follow the easy path offered by her wealthy family, but to use her money, her beauty, her charm, and her brain to do something extraordinary with her life. In this book I focus on Victoria Ocampo, the feminist, whose essays on women deserve to bring her even more significance and distinction. For it is my belief that what is most notable about Ocampo and gives her feminism a strong appeal is her fundamental humanism and her constructive view of the relationship between men and women. It is my hope that *Victoria Ocampo: Writer, Feminist, Women of the World* will introduce this complex woman to a new and broader audience of "common readers," both male and female.

Sources

In an effort to be helpful to the reader, I have identified, in the text, the sources that originate with Ocampo as well as other sources which are used more than twice. (For example, A,6:127 refers to the autobiography, volume 6, and DM:45

refers to the biography by Doris Meyer). For a select group of Ocampo's essays, I have identified each one with a number (E-1, E-2, and so on) and, in the Abbreviations that are found on pages xi–xii, I have given each one its Spanish title and source. (Those that have been published in English translation are indicated by an asterisk and information about the translation is given as a section of the bibliography on pages 184–85.) Page references in the text refer to the essay in Spanish. All other sources will be found in the endnotes and will be identified in the usual manner.

Acknowledgments

I am very greatly indebted to Doris Meyer for her 1979 biography of Ocampo. It has been a continually helpful source of information. Additionally, she has shown extreme generosity in lending me many of her photographs of Victoria Ocampo for use in this book. I would like to thank Janet Greenberg, whose doctoral thesis on Ocampo has been both useful and provocative. I am grateful to Beatriz Sarlo for the insights she gave me in her short essay on Ocampo, and to John King for his careful and informative study of *Sur*. I have benefited from comments on earlier drafts by Susan Darrow, Ina Sandalow, and Alison Steiner.

Two libraries deserve acknowledgment. The first is the Houghton Library at Harvard University, where I spent several days reading in their collection of Ocampo's correspondence (bMS Span 117). All citations from the Victoria Ocampo papers are published by permission of the Houghton Library, Harvard University. The Harlan Hatcher Graduate Library at the University of Michigan is a place I have always approached as a "temple" and which through the years has kept me well supplied with the books I need.

My special thanks go to Barbara Guth, my editor at the University of New Mexico Press. She has been unfailingly gracious and intelligent every step of the way in the long process of making this book a reality.

Finally, my thanks to my husband, Peter O. Steiner. He has been my critic, my editor, and, still, my greatest friend.

Abbreviations

* A title followed by an asterisk (*) indicates that this essay has been previously published
in an English translation. Details of the translations will be found in the bibliography on page 184.

The only thing that counts is what each of us has done with our life after the accident of our birth . . . whether we have taken advantage of our opportunities or not, how we have struggled to overcome the obstacles that beset us.

VICTORIA OCAMPO

PART ONE

The Education of Victoria Ocampo

(1890–1931)

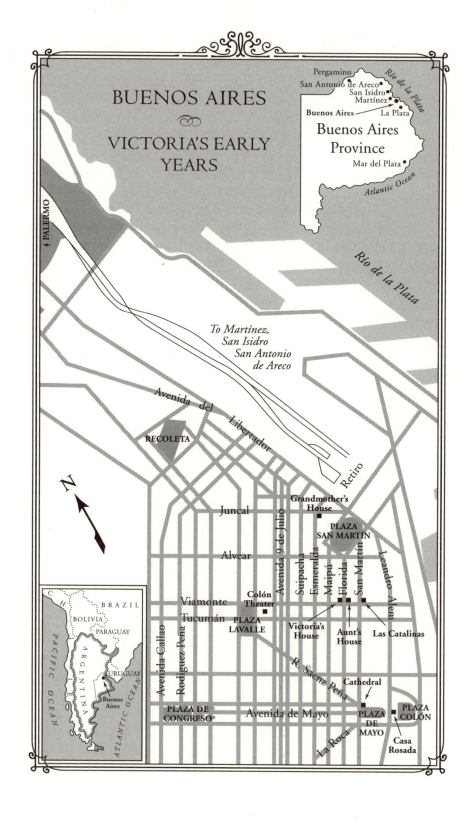

BUENOS AIRES

VICTORIA'S EARLY YEARS

Buenos Aires
Province

Pergamino
San Antonio de Areco
San Isidro
Martínez
Buenos Aires
La Plata

Río de la Plata

Mar del Plata

Atlantic Ocean

PALERMO

Río de la Plata

To Martínez,
San Isidro
San Antonio
de Areco

Avenida del

Libertador

RECOLETA

Retiro

N

Grandmother's
House

Juncal

PLAZA
SAN MARTÍN

Avenida 9 de Julio

Alvear

Suipacha
Esmeralda
Maipú
Florida
San Martín

Leandro Alem

Viamonte

Colón
Theater

Tucumán

PLAZA
LAVALLE

Victoria's
House

Aunt's
House

Las Catalinas

BRAZIL

BOLIVIA

PARAGUAY

CHILE

ARGENTINA

URUGUAY

Buenos
Aires

PACIFIC
OCEAN

ATLANTIC
OCEAN

Avenida Callao
Rodríguez Peña

R. Sáenz Peña

Cathedral

PLAZA DE
CONGRESO

Avenida de Mayo

La Roca

PLAZA
DE
MAYO

PLAZA
COLÓN

Casa
Rosada

CHAPTER ONE ∾ EARLY YEARS

Victoria was born in Buenos Aires in 1890, a time of horse-drawn carriages when girls from wealthy families were usually given a gentle education at home by governesses. Chances were that such a girl would have a proper courtship followed by an approved marriage to some young man from an equally prominent family. She would then grow gracefully into a life of quiet domesticity under the watchful eye of her family and the Catholic Church. A contented life perhaps, punctuated by successive births, an active social life, charity events, and an occasional trip to Europe, but a life that was "a happy prison," one that would usually preclude an independent intellectual existence.[1]

From the beginning Victoria reacted to this world around her—a tight circle of protective family surrounded by luxury but circumscribed by taboos, censorship, and prohibitions.

Childhood

Victoria opened her autobiography with glimpses of herself before she was seven. From her perspective as a woman of sixty-two it was like entering a dream world, one that sometimes came back "with the speed of perfume." It was like those dreams that "we never manage to piece together once we've awakened . . . and from which we only recall an atmosphere of anguish or happiness. My first recollections emerge in my conscious memory as a capricious archipelago in an ocean of oblivion" (A,1:68,65).

It was a long archipelago that stretched from Buenos Aires to her grandparents' ranches where Victoria spent summers with her sisters, and to Paris, London, and Italy where they lived in hotels for a year. Many of the islands from this remembered archipelago offer insights into the young Victoria Ocampo. She acknowledged that she saw in these early memories certain reflections of her personality: indignation in response to injustice and cruelty, impassioned tenderness for those she loved, an interest in food, fear of seeing people cry, dread of revealing her pain or sorrow, an intentional act of dissimulation whenever she was suffering, tremendous pleasure in physical beauty (A,1:66).

She might also have added that her memories showed early signs of the rebelliousness and tendency to violence that would show up in her later life. But

3

mostly the picture that Victoria gave of herself was of a pampered little girl with the normal mix of naughtiness and wonder. What was special to Victoria at this young age was a certain precocious self-assurance, an uneasy deference to males, a keen eye for details, a delight in things sensuous, and that heightened sense of the dramatic that would punctuate her life and writing.

FIRST MEMORIES[2]

The Well

I climbed up on something to get to the well. I peered over the top at the water. I shouted. The well shouted back. I shouted again. I thought it was fun. No one in the patio. I was the boss of the patio.

Soon I looked up and saw Grandpa Ocampo[3] standing in the doorway of his room. He raised his cane, threatening me it seemed . . . He didn't like my getting up on the well. He wanted me to get down right away.

He came toward me, without using his cane. First I felt surprise, then indignation and fear. Indignation, above all, overwhelmed me. The cane! Why had he raised it? I couldn't believe what I was seeing. I got down fast and I don't know how. I ran. I ran to my Aunt Vitola's room. She was on the bed with a kerchief tied around her forehead. Sobbing, I threw myself on the bed. I cried to her: "Grandpa Ocampo wants to hit me."

The Horse

As we came home from our daily excursion to Palermo, I saw a horse tied to a tree in a vacant lot on Alvear Avenue. A man was whipping it. The horse, driven crazy by the whipping, was trying to escape by pulling away, but he only ended up by winding himself around the tree. There was no way for him to escape.

Once again, like the day of the well and Grandpa Ocampo's cane, I felt overwhelmed. I wanted to cry. I was trembling. It seemed to me that I couldn't go on living if that whipping didn't stop. When I got back to the house I wanted to run to the corner to tell the policeman what had happened. That's what I did.

The Cake

I'm sitting up in bed, wrapped in an enormous towel. I've just had a bath. My hair is wet. Ina, my nursemaid, is giving me little pieces of cake. I hardly breathe so I won't lose a crumb. I'm tasting that kind of cake for the first time.

Tata Ocampo Has Gone To Heaven

One morning Papa came to my room and said: "Grandpa Ocampo has gone to heaven." Right away I sense that those words are hiding something terrible. I say nothing. I want Papa to believe that I believe what he is saying and that it seems natural to me that he is coming here just to tell me. I'm afraid of going back to my aunts. They're going to cry a lot and people who cry frighten me.

Paloma

My cousin Paloma is sitting on the stairs in the second patio. We've been fighting. She's sitting with her back to me. Without letting her see me and without making any noise, I creep up on her and hit her on the head with all my might. I know it's bad to do that. I'm ashamed because I've crept up on her. I'm ashamed, but I hit her anyway.

Imperfection

My sister Angélica and I are walking along the Avenue of the Casuarina with Pepito and Eduardo. I adore Pepito. He's two years older than me. We'll get married some day. He brings me sugar cubes in his pockets. I walk in front with him.

Behind us, the nursemaids and two other children are coming. "Look," Pepito says to me. He keeps walking and unbuttons his short pants. He shows me a little piece of rosy flesh. I look, too surprised to ask questions. Pepito seems proud of what he's showing me. That ridiculous object he showed me bothers me. Because I do think it's ridiculous. But because it's Pepito I don't tell him that I don't like it. Pepito fastens his pants again.

We don't talk about this business any more. I think the little piece of rosy flesh makes him ugly. But what am I going to do? His face is so lovely that I end up pardoning him for his imperfection.

Patios

There are three patios in my grandparent's house. I escape to them when I can, especially to the one in the middle that smells of flowers and to the one in back because Francisca is there. Francisca is black like Juan Allende. She spends hours sitting there, slowly smoothing pieces of brown paper between her hands. Afterwards she puts them in the bathroom. This seems an enviable job to me. I like Francisca very much.

Darkness

Darkness, night, frighten me. At times I can't stand it. I run to Mama's room as if something or someone were chasing me. If she lets me stay in her bed for a while it goes away. Nothing bad can happen to me now.

Book

I hold a book that they read to me earlier and I pretend that I'm reading it. I remember the story perfectly and I understand what's behind the letters that I don't know.[4]

Manias

I can't go to sleep if someone—my great aunt Madrina if possible—isn't holding my hand. I put my hand under her cuff where the skin is soft. That's how I like to go to sleep. (A,I:75–82)

EARLY EXPERIENCES

Little Girls

[When I was six and we were in Paris] I went up to a little blond girl in Pré Catelan Park because I liked her face so much. I said to her in French: "Do you want to play with me?" Now we play together whenever I go there. She makes a game out of looking for little frogs. She keeps them in a cardboard box with little holes so they can breathe. I begin to look for little frogs too.

Bois de Boulogne

When we walk near the lake in the Bois de Boulogne they buy us stale bread for the ducks and swans. I like it better than regular white bread. I eat it when nobody's looking. (A,I:82–83)

La Place de La Concorde

Madrina asks me: "What would you like me to buy you as a souvenir of Paris?" On the Rue de la Paix at Cartier's I've seen a ring with a ruby that looks like one of Boissier's square raspberry caramels. I say: "The ruby from Cartier." Madrina answers: "It isn't a ring for little girls. What else would you like?" Then I say: "Give me a big photograph of La Place de la Concorde?" (A,I:88)

London

The soaps are round and made of glycerin. You can play with them in the bathtub. In the hotel there's an official dressed in red with a wand under his arm and a little round hat tilted to one side of his head. He is tall and blonde and elegant.

My Namesake

Today is the saint's day of Queen Victoria, my namesake. We've been a long time on the balcony, watching soldiers parade by. The streets are full of people. We are waiting, waiting for the queen to pass by. I'm tired and bored. Finally a beautiful coach arrives. Inside, a fat old lady. Nothing more. They call this a Jubilee. (A,1:87)

In 1897 the Ocampos returned to Argentina by ship and one of Victoria's uncles met them in Mar del Plata. Once back home Victoria couldn't believe that the street where she had lived looked so narrow and ugly. It couldn't be the same wide street she had left only a year ago. Victoria dreaded going to see her aunts for the first time. She was afraid she would betray herself with some show of emotion.

My aunts are waiting for me. I don't want them to see my heart. I have to distract them, to make them believe that I'm thirsty, that I'm hungry, that I'm sleepy. If they kiss me, I'm done for. I'm going to cry and I don't want to, I don't want to. It's as if some danger were threatening me. They ask me if I'm happy to be back. I answer: "Could I have some water with a honey roll?" I haven't forgotten the white honey rolls with the taste of lemon and sugar. They say: "Poor little thing, she's thirsty." . . .

My great aunt Vitola was waiting for me with a doll and her trunk full of outfits just as if the doll were a real little girl. Vitola made all the clothes herself, the hats, the white dresses. It was a doll with all the same things I had. Little sets of underwear, aprons, socks. I always dressed her in the simplest clothes. I said to Vitola: "When I'm a big girl and I go to a dance, I'll put on a white dress with no decoration and a belt of real pearls. I like simple things."

I speak better French than Spanish and I like it more. How did that happen? A very old Mademoiselle comes to give us French lessons. After five minutes I say to her: "I'll be right back. In a minute." I don't come back.

In the afternoons Aunt Mercedes washes strawberries to make ice cream. The plates are white with a rose border. She puts the clean fruit in a food mill and mashes it with a white wooden spoon. Out comes a rich, red cream

that bit by bit fills the bowl. I don't take my eyes off it. When Aunt Mercedes finishes, I know she'll let me lick the spoon.

Twice a week Grandmother changes the flowers in the vases. She brings
them from San Isidro in big baskets. There's a special room for arranging
them; it always has such a wonderful smell! Grandmother makes bouquets
of all the smells.

⚬⚬⚬

You can't go up on the rooftop on Florida and Viamonte without special permission and without holding someone's hand. The little stairway
up to it is narrow and dark. But when the door opens it's dazzling. There's
so much light and so much sky! So much space! Below, you can see the
patios, and the neighbors' patios too. But they won't let you get near the edge
to have a good look. . . .

I like to stay alone in the big, closed-up, half-dark rooms when nobody's
around. Most of all in summertime when all the chairs have white cloth
draped over them and the floors are covered with straw-colored matting.
Hardly a speck of sun comes in through the iron grilles on the windows and
the green Persian blinds. I walk on tip-toe so I won't spoil the silence; I
can hear it. In the daytime I like the silence, but it makes me afraid at night.
The silence of the rooms in summer smells of flowers from San Isidro and
straw mats. (A,I:89–92)

Every day they took Angélica and me from the house on Viamonte to
spend the day in our great aunts' house. We came back home at night to
eat and sleep. Sometimes when we got home, they let us go into the dining room for a few minutes while Papa and Mama were eating. They always
had lettuce salad and I would escape to the pantry to fish some lettuce out
of the salad bowl. (They never let me eat lettuce because it's a raw vegetable.)

Mama was very pretty and I liked to look at her when she got all dressed
up for the theater. I liked Papa too. To look at him. (A,I:94)

In 1890 Victoria's grandparents had built Villa Ocampo in San Isidro, in the
suburbs. Throughout her long life Victoria's strong attachment to San Isidro
and the family estate there gave her a firm and healthy sense of place.

When we go to San Isidro in December I sleep in the room next to my
great aunts, Vitola and Carmen. Vitola sits down by my bed and almost
every night she reads me fairy stories before she puts out the light. But she
always leaves a night light on because I'm afraid of the dark. As soon as

Vitola has gone to bed I begin calling to her: "Until tomorrow, Vitola." From her room she answers: "Until tomorrow, kitty-cat." This goes on and on until Vitola gets tired and doesn't answer. Then my fervor grows and with it my desire to make her repeat, just one more time, "Until tomorrow, kitty-cat." She has to be the last one to say it. If not, I'm not at peace. This ceremony takes place every night. Sometimes Vitola gets stubborn and doesn't answer. She thinks I insist too much. Then, what a problem! I can't keep quiet, but I don't want to displease her. No. I can't abandon the game until I hear her say "Until tomorrow, kitty-cat."

One afternoon, in the garden at Villa Ocampo, I ate some rare fruit that people don't usually eat and that had a bad taste. I had picked it off a thorny bush that grew beside the door. I asked Don Francisco, the gardener, what it was called. He didn't tell me, but he warned me that it was poison.

As soon as it was night, Don Francisco's voice started growing inside me. Poison, **Poison, POISON.** I couldn't think of anything else. I was poisoned. I was going to die. I was going to die that very night. As soon as I got into bed I said "Until tomorrow" to Vitola and a tremendous wave of terror overcame me. I had kissed Vitola for the last time. It would be better if she didn't know. If I told her, it would be worse. I had to keep my silence. I tossed around in bed. I couldn't find any position that seemed suitable for waiting for death. When would I start to feel it? How long would I have to wait for it? Where on my body would it begin?

Vitola, in the other room, heard that I was restless, which was unusual for me, and came in to see what was going on. My night shirt was drenched in sweat. This surprised her. She asked me if I hurt anywhere. I told her I wanted to go pee-pee.

Her being there was a relief, but I was resolved not to tell her anything. She put another night shirt on me. She told me it was time to go to sleep, that day was already dawning. Day was dawning? There would be light? But then I'm not going to die, I thought. Nobody dies in the daytime. By the time Vitola left my room, light was already coming in through the Persian blinds. Day! I hugged my pillow and, exhausted, I fell asleep.

There are swans in a little pond at San Isidro. When you go to the water's edge to have a good look at them—although you don't talk to them the way you would to a dog or a cat; they wouldn't understand—they spread their wings with rage, and they rise up with their long necks, ready to bite you. They are wicked, even though they're so white. But the more their wings swell up, the more I want to make them get out of the water. I realize that they're going to chase me. They are very, very bad. But I run faster on grass than they do.

❧

After tea at San Isidro our nursemaids wash our hands and faces and change our clothes. They always put us in white dresses with wide sashes made of different colored heavy ribbons. They keep the ribbons in place by fastening them to a pleat with a pin. I'm always afraid that it's going to pinch my belly button so I don't breathe and I try to pull in my stomach as much as I can. Afterwards, when we're all sweet and clean, we go back to the garden, but "not to run wild." Our clothes come from one of Vitola's wardrobes that smells of sachets and some Indian spice. I'm more comfortable in the aprons I wear in the morning. They don't have as much starch.

We have a lot of toys. But my great aunt Rosa is the keeper of the toys. She says we ruin them in no time, so she had a cupboard made with glass doors where she keeps the toys locked up—not all of them, just the nicest ones. There's a blond doll dressed in a green velvet suit with gold braid that is marvellous and very big. It isn't a woman, it's a man, with long pants. On the twenty-fifth of May and the ninth of July and other important days the toy cupboard is opened; the doll has to see the soldiers parade by too. Sometimes I make them let me take him for a ride in the carriage. Then I shout at him: "Breathe! Breathe! Before you know it Rosa will put you back in jail." I hope that when Rosa hears this or finds out I'm saying it, she'll get angry. (A,1:96–101)

Both sets of Victoria's grandparents had ranches in Argentina, so when summer came Victoria went with her sisters to one of these ranches or to Villa Ocampo. Of her time on the ranches she recalled:

. . . sheep, alfalfa, ostrich and tero eggs, cousins . . . rides in a little carriage, toasted hardtack, sometimes mate [tea], buckets of foamy milk, my aunt Isabel playing waltzes on an upright piano, warnings such as "I've already told you not to hide the boy's cap" (the boy was crying) . . . bruises on my knees, mud on my hands ("Can't you stay clean for even one second?"), laughter, tears, races, reading. (A,1:12,13)

When we go to Pergamino to the ranch named La Rabona, my sisters and I have another diversion besides the little cart pulled by two woolly lambs. We play with our young cousins, Martin and Roberto. I always fight with Martin and I always want to hit him. His cherubic face makes me mad because he says bad things with this face. If I could, sometimes I think I'd strangle him.

Evaristo, the man who brought bags of hardtack into the house at La Rabona, was a very handsome young man. I admired him. He would talk with the nursemaids while we were playing. He certainly didn't look at me the way he looked at the nursemaids. It was a very happy thing to be a nursemaid at La Rabona. (A,1:101)

LESSONS

One day they announced to my sister Angélica and me that an instructress had just arrived. They say she knows many things, is strict and won't let me go into tirades the way I've been doing. They tell me I'm old enough now not to do everything I want to. (Or, I ask, is it that I'm still not old enough to do everything I want?) Mademoiselle will give us French lessons every morning from nine to eleven. She will stay for lunch. At one she will take us to Palermo Park where we will play and we will sit on a bench and study our lessons for the following day. Slavery. Slavery is named Alexandrine Bonnemason. She is French, naturally. A relative of ours recommended her to Vitola, saying: "She is a well of science." This recommendation doesn't make me very enthusiastic. I have no intention of converting myself into a well of science. Nor do I want anyone to try to convert me into one.

The first day of class I tried to play my usual trick: "Wait a minute. I'll be right back." But they didn't let me leave the room. Vitola has told Mademoiselle that she shouldn't put up with any foolishness, that she should make me study hard, showing no mercy. Vitola! She wants me to learn lots of things. She keeps watch over me. But Mademoiselle absolutely has to give me two minutes to go to the bathroom (where I lock myself in to watch the flies buzzing around or to smell the soap). Vitola confronts me: "What is all this wasting of time?" She knows perfectly well that I go to the bathroom to escape. Then I throw myself in her arms, I kiss her: "Vitola, Vitola!" I plead. Nothing. She doesn't give in. Mademoiselle's lessons and Mademoiselle herself immediately take an important place in my life and in my sister's life.

Mademoiselle begins by putting me in jail because I answer back. How can I not answer back? She won't let us speak except when she asks a question about our lessons. She makes us make the sign of the cross and say an Our Father and a Hail Mary before the beginning of class and she does it with us. She repeats, apropos of whatever, as a threat: "This is the last time I am going to repeat this to you." (A,1:102–3)

Occasionally Mademoiselle punished me by standing me up with my arms stretched out, in the form of a cross, with a book in each hand. Or sometimes she threatened us with a dunce's cap made from an old newspaper. (A,1:114)

Every day after lunch a rented coupe comes to take us to Palermo. . . . Near Recoleta the street is full of puddles. When we get to one I shout at the driver, Eustacio, "Straight through the water, Eustacio, straight through the water." The coupe jounces and we bounce around, enchanted.

Sometimes when we pass by a corner in front of a policeman, I shout at him . . . and I show him my naked doll through the carriage window, to see if he gets mad. But he doesn't pay any attention. My cousin, Paloma, told me that the nuns at her school have warned her to cover the mirrors in the bathroom when she takes a bath. Is that because it's a sin to be naked?

❧

We are learning La Fontaine's fables. They don't bore me the way arithmetic does. I've decided not to learn arithmetic. When we have to do one of the four fundamental operations, I copy whatever Angélica has put down in her notebook, changing some number at random so they won't discover my trick. But Mademoiselle isn't deceived and gives us different assignments. Mademoiselle recites verses from memory. Racine and Corneille. She takes off her glasses and wipes her eyes before she begins. I could listen to her for hours. (A,1:105–6)

Our English governess, Miss Ellis, had a wonderful smell, clean clothes, and starched blouses. I learned English quickly, by ear, I guess. I learned to read it too. Miss Ellis always went around carrying magazines full of pictures of people and she brought us chocolate bonbons. She didn't frighten us the way Mademoiselle did. The nursery rhymes and Miss Ellis's stories were fun. She talked continually about Queen Victoria and the royal family. She showed us photographs of the family in magazines. The Transvaal and the Boers worried her. The English people didn't like them, nor did the Boers like the English. I began to like the Boers. . . .

Miss Ellis told us about how they had Christmas in England with snow; and about St. Leonard's, the convent where she went to school. Sometimes she took us to the English shops on Cangallo Street. In the shops she talked about the Boer War, in English. I overheard: "It's a shame."

I didn't get good grades in my English lessons and even though I was on my good behavior, Miss Ellis complained to my parents. . . . She told them that she wasn't happy about my not studying, that I distracted my sister from her work by making all kinds of faces. She complained that my sister, who was more serious than I, but younger, was my victim. She said I was the one who was misbehaving; naturally I was the one who got blamed for everything. I got a long, serious scolding from my father.

Charged with indignation and rage . . . and not knowing how to get even, I began to write. I wrote a protest accusing Miss Ellis of being a tattletale for telling on me. . . . I wrote that the English were cowards because they wanted to wipe out the poor Boers; I wrote that Miss Ellis wanted a complete victory over the Boers in Africa; I wrote that she was all in favor of putting an end to the British Empire. Finally, I jumped on what people had done to Joan of Arc. . . . I discovered that to write was a relief. This was the beginning of my literary career. (A,I:112–13)

Miss Ellis, who never was able to tame the wild pony in me, was very different from Mademoiselle. I never saw her in a rage. Except for the day when she spoke to my father, she never again complained, although she had plenty of reason. We got along fine. Better than anyone she understood what Christmas was. She told us lots and lots of stories, she showed us pictures of England that made me think I'd like to live there. Through her very presence, her super-clean, starched blouses, her scent of lavender, her big, clear handwriting, her crackers, her butterscotch, her magazines, her umbrella, England entered into our classroom. I soon forgot about her going to my parents with complaints, to try to get from me what she never succeeded in getting: my attention when I wasn't amused or interested. (A,I:115)

Victoria remembered learning to play the piano as a torment. She hated practicing scales, she was bothered by not being able to look at the keyboard, and she didn't like her teacher, Berta Krauss, who was even more severe than Mademoiselle.

Berta Krauss took a look at our hands and fingernails. Our hands weren't very big. She wanted them to conform but she couldn't make them suddenly grow larger. Instead she said our fingernails were too long and that we should cut them as short as possible. I didn't like this idea. I never, never let my fingernails be cut very short. . . . My fingernails belonged to me and I didn't see how anyone had any right to make me cut my fingernails to be like Danish ones. (A,I:120–21)

When we went to Miss Krauss's house, (she sometimes held recitals there) we discovered that Miss Krauss smoked. This astounded us. We had never seen a woman smoke although Madrina, who had traveled in Russia, the United States, and Egypt, once said that somewhere she had been the women smoked cigars. All of Miss Krauss's students liked to whisper about this discovery of ours. (A,I:123)

INTROSPECTION

Primogeniture

There were no secrets between Angélica and me (how could there be?). We understood each other in half words. We wore the same dresses, the same hats, the same shoes. Mine were bigger, but that was all. We read the same books at the same time, we studied the same geography, the same grammar, at the same time. We went everywhere together, I in front and she behind.[5] We went into the same shops, I in front and she behind. We got into the same carriages, I in front and she behind. We climbed the same stairs, I in front and she behind.

My right of primogeniture, that right so commented on by the *Histoire Sainte* which we were studying, seemed to me indisputable and natural. I would have considered it absurd to live in any other way than I in front and she behind. That order began when we were born. I demanded obedience and offered protection. But at night when one of those immense deserts of endless fear overcame me in my bed and I felt completely lost, it was I who reached over to the next bed and woke Angélica: "Are you sleeping?" I sought her hand, and once I had that smaller, weaker hand (the same hand that during the day I had perhaps pressed too hard either out of distraction or violence), the enemy darkness seemed less threatening.

"Courage"

Pretending to skate on the patios on Tucuman Street, I had the bright idea of putting soap on the bottoms of my shoes; I slipped and fell on my left arm. I felt a sharp pain and wasn't able to move my arm. I had to hold it up with the other arm. This happened after lunch when it was time to go to Palermo. Despite the pain, I left as usual, without saying anything to my aunts. By the time we got to the park my arm was swollen. I put it under a faucet with cold water. The pain was getting worse. We were starting home when we met Mother up by Recoleta. She signaled the driver to stop our carriage and getting down from her own carriage, asked: "What is the matter with this child?" She had seen my distraught face. I told her: "I fell skating and now I can't move my arm." She took me into her carriage and we went to the house of Doctor Alejandro Castro, who had the reputation in our family (he was a relative) of being a very good doctor. Then, besides having pain, I was afraid.

Who knows what they were going to do to me. The fact that Alejandro Castro was a great surgeon alarmed me a whole lot more. If it required so much scientific expertise, it was because they considered my case to be critical, I thought. The great doctor looked at me and felt my arm all over without my letting out even a peep. He made a sign to my mother and they went off together. They talked. Things began to look more serious for me. What were they talking about? They returned, smiling, like accomplices. He announced to me: "We'll get these bones back in place and your arm won't hurt you any more." He added that I could cry if I wanted to, if it hurt me. He began to pull on my arm. The pain was horrible, but my fear was stronger than everything else. It made me keep quiet. If this doctor knew about my pain, he would cut off my arm as a cure. That's what doctors did. Finally my martyrdom came to an end. The doctor, so tranquil and with such a sure hand, put a splint on my arm and bandaged it. Then he said to Mama: "You have a very brave daughter." It wasn't true. I had not cried out of cowardice. On the ride back home, Mama told me that the way I had behaved had astounded her. She said I had two broken bones, the radius and the cubitus, and the doctor had set them so they would knit together again. The resetting was extremely painful, and I hadn't made a murmur. From fear, I thought. From fear I would let myself be killed without a murmur. . . .

I spent a month with my arm immobilized and taking advantage of the chance to do whatever I wanted. In this way I exploited the fact that I hadn't cried. My reputation for being brave promoted me to a higher plateau. It gave me new privileges. "The poor little thing didn't even complain. And they say that she's spoiled!" The poor little thing knew perfectly well why she hadn't complained.

Lita

Two of our relatives lived in [the nearby town of] Martínez, in a house with a garden that you approached through an avenue of eucalyptus. They were young ladies of perfect beauty who already went to dances and had boyfriends: María Florentina and Lita. I liked Lita best and could have spent hours and hours just thinking about her.

Almost every afternoon in the summertime when we'd go for a ride in the carriage, I'd say to Chacho: "Go by Lita's house." . . . Lita was an enchanted princess. Sometimes she would appear in flesh and blood, in the distance, in the garden. . . . One day she had the carriage stop and invited us in for a visit. She was wearing a beige dress. When I got close to her I could see that her cheeks were without a trace of color, but as if illuminated from within. I remember those big, dark, sparkling eyes, and the whiteness of her smile, the black hair drawn into a bun at the back of her neck. Lita was tall and of a *taille elancee,* as Mademoiselle would say. She had a languor as she walked that was very much her own. . . .

Lita took a walk through the garden with me. If Venus (we were now at the height of my mythological phase) had come down from Olympus and the Virgin Mary from heaven just to please me, I couldn't have felt more moved. Passing by a rosebush she cut a rose for me. I can see her cutting it, her head bending over and her skirt getting caught on some thorns. Paralyzed by what I saw, I didn't even try to free her from the wicked rosebush. Reverently I would have touched the hem of that beige skirt and I would have gotten my fingers pricked getting her loose from the thorn. I would have wanted to hold back the sun, like Joshua, stopping time, just so Lita would stay forever cutting a rose and I would be centuries looking at her cutting it, in a garden in Martínez. Later I put the rose in my missal. Things like that were not of this earth. (A,1:129–34)

Music

I had an aunt, Mercedes, . . . who often played the piano at home. And rather well. She had studied in Paris. . . . Her turned-up nose didn't seem to go with the sad pieces she usually played. To me her favorite music seemed desperately passionate, melancholy, and violent. But I liked it; I preferred it. . . . Everything about this music reached out to my heart. . . . Sitting on a chair as close as possible to the piano, I would follow the comings and goings of her fingers, hypnotized by the sounds. I could have cried at times because some passages of the impromptus, of the ballads, of the etudes, of the mazurkas, of the preludes, were so moving. It seemed to me that the music was pressing on my heart until it changed my heart's shape. Or, perhaps, on the contrary, that it was encircling my heart until it discovered its own shape, in sorrowful pleasure.

Inequality

When we moved to a new house, Madrina gave me some furniture for my room. For the first time in my life I was going to sleep alone. My bedroom, with beautiful yellow silk curtains, a prayer stool, and a Virgin to pray to, seemed perfect to me. To begin in a new house was like trying on the new dresses, hats, and shoes that arrived every spring and fall from Paris in great white wooden boxes. Those clothes smelled of Paris the way the new house smelled of new wood and fresh paint. I loved the smell of our new house.

After we moved I became aware for the first time of the problem of wealth and poverty. The change made me take a close look at things that I had never noticed before. I suppose that I had accepted the comfort and luxury that surrounded me, the way a bird accepts his nest—without knowing how it was made or whether other birds had similar kinds of nests. But the experience of living in unfamiliar rooms forced me to realize that those rooms were luxurious. One night while Micaela was braiding my hair, in my new bedroom, I said to her: "If it were up to me there wouldn't be any rich people or any poor people, do you know that?" (A,1:135–19)

BOYS

In summer, three boys came to San Isidro to spend their vacations at our house: Juancito, Alfredo and Franky. Juancito and Alfredo were the sons of Juan Allende, now dead, my great grandfather's incomparable house servant, a capable, hard-working, trustworthy black. . . .

Franky was the son of Gathy, Madrina's English (or Irish?) servant. Blond, with very white skin covered with freckles, he had beautiful blue eyes. The three boys played games of tops, "rescue," cops and robbers, and croquet with us girls. Juancito and Alfredo liked me and were obedient subjects, but I admired Franky and I went out of my way to try to please him. I played the games he liked best, I saved part of my cake for him (indisputable proof of my love). But Franky was not easily buttered up and he showed no sign that he appreciated such scandalous privileges.

There was only one time when I felt accepted by him as an equal. We were playing hide and seek and I had hidden with him behind the greenhouse in a huge pot of plants with very large leaves. (I had found it and I considered it a magnificent hiding place.) Crouching down, side by side, not even breathing, we could hear Juancito and Alfredo running around trying to find us. Franky had never before been so tolerant of me. He had never before agreed to hide with me. But that moment of triumph and happiness lasted only a short time: the curly heads of our playmates soon peeked through the green leaves. The hiding place was not, after all, as good as I had claimed, Franky said. Franky didn't have a high opinion of girls, a thing that offended me and made me sad beyond measure. . . . Franky didn't even recognize what had become obvious. His indifference, his inhumane coldness, his aggressive independence were tearing my heart to pieces and eating away at my self-esteem. I liked him in spite of his mean words and I would have been proud to have freckles like his. Everything about him seemed enviable. In winter, these boys disappeared from our lives.

[Somewhat later] one of my mother's sisters died and left seven children in my grandmother's charge. They spent the summer at the neighboring estate in San Isidro. The croquet games with this new contingent took on more importance. I immediately began to admire my cousin C., seven years older than I. He treated me with complete disdain, even more so than Franky. I didn't exist for him. Nevertheless, I did things on a equal footing with the boys (there were four of them) and I even beat them at croquet. But this didn't seem to count. C. didn't even realize it. I resigned myself to my sad fate. It was clear that I wasn't able to impress boys. . . . During the winter I saw C. at my grandmother's house where he lived with his brothers and sisters. Her house on Suipacha Street [in Buenos Aires] . . . was very large, perfect for playing hide and seek. But C. didn't play hiding games and was not a playmate for us. The hard look in his blue eyes, the short, ironic tone he adopted, his long pants—all this made him an absolutely inaccessible, remote human being. I contemplated him as if he were the summit of a glacier. Or an iceberg being pulled by the current to other shores. He had a scornful way of laughing that gave me goose flesh. If he had suspected my childish infatuation, how he would have laughed. I didn't even want to imagine it.

In a small room where they stored old junk, C. said he liked to do chemistry experiments. He worked with rare instruments and batteries. He would sometimes call all of us younger children to that room, stand us in a line and then, taking us by the hand, he would make an electric current, that was stored in his own hand, pass right through that chain of trembling, obedient flesh. I went along with his disagreeable experiment just to prove to him that I wasn't afraid and also because it was an unexpected privilege, a concession from that superior being, to receive an electric charge that had passed through C.'s hand. When he finished the experiment and had dazzled us with his great knowledge, C. would dispatch us without a word of thanks and close the door in our faces. I would leave that room with all its junk as if I were tied to him by an elastic which pulled on me more and more as I went away.

My insignificance to C. crushed my spirit. And his indifference (that was the worst) seemed unbearable to me and yet justified, cruel and natural, all at the same time. One day as I was with my mother going down the long, steep stairway at the Suipacha house, I had the feeling that I was going to throw myself right down the stairs and roll onto the crimson carpet or that I was going to go running back to the room of the experiments to shout at C. that I was a human being too and that he couldn't treat me like an old rag. (A,I:139–43)

MENSTRUATION

My much older cousin Clarita, my father's cousin really, had given us some books that she read when she was our age. Books with red covers and gold lettering, fairy tales. I noticed that at the beginning of a few of them someone had tried, without success, to cover up some of the words with ink. But I could still read: "The queen became large and gave the world a princess."

⁂

When I went home one night (I had spent the day as usual at my aunts' house), I was surprised by my mother's appearance. She seemed to be completely deformed. She wasn't the same as before. I had a sense of uneasiness, of distress, of rebelliousness seeing her in that condition, different. As if someone had stolen her away from me. I looked at her with animosity and fear. Fear because it seemed to me that she was in danger. Animosity because that fear was making me suffer. I was sure now that this was the way babies began, by that deformation. When my fourth sister had been born in Paris they told me that babies came from Paris. . . . As time went by the mystery of birth aroused both my apprehension and curiosity; I was in a state of recurring anguish. "The queen became large." . . . Could I possibly doubt, as I looked at my mother, that the same thing was happening to her? And that a baby would be born, I didn't know how, although I imagined that it would come out through the belly button and that they would tell me that

it came from Paris. That little round hole hidden in the middle of the stomach couldn't be for anything else. It appalled me to think about how the skin
would have to break so that a baby, however minuscule it might be, would
be able to make its way through that tiny opening. How horrible. Why
weren't babies born in a less atrocious way? Like chickens, for example?
Or like oranges that had something like the beginning of a little orange in
their navels? Mothers were like oranges. But that a navel would burst apart
seemed monstrously cruel; I was overcome with panic.

⁋

One day, as I was doing up my underpants in the bathroom, I saw that
they were spotted with red. And my undershirt too. It was blood. I wondered where it could have come from because nothing sharp had scratched
me, nothing had cut my legs (something that happened to me with a certain
regularity). Besides, I didn't climb fences and trees in winter the way I did
in summer. I called Micaela and said: "Look at my undershirt. I'm bleeding. . . . What is this?" She told me to wait a minute and went off to find
Mama. Mama told me that the blood wasn't anything in particular. That
declaration didn't satisfy me—I knew my mother was just trying to play
down the importance of something quite upsetting for me. She added that
my cousin M. had that too, just like all girls who arrive at an age when they
begin to be señoritas. That, every month. She told me you couldn't take a
bath in cold water while it lasted, nor play with cold water, nor get your
legs wet. That you had to use lukewarm water and that you didn't talk about
those things in front of men. With women, yes. Neither, for the moment,
should I talk about that to my younger sisters.

To me, all this business seemed strange, disagreeable in the extreme,
and on top of it all, humiliating. Why did I have to be quiet about that? Was
it perhaps a shameful thing? . . . Suddenly I felt as if I were imprisoned by
a chance of fate that I rejected with all my powers. I'd run away! But how
to run away from my own body? . . . I suffered terribly because they made
me feel ashamed of something that wasn't my fault and that had nothing
to do with my own free will.

I went from depression to the most furious rebellion. Cowering within
myself, as if to offer the smallest possible target, I felt I was a prisoner of
my body. Of my body that I hated because it was betraying me by acting
in such an unexpected way. . . . People were forcing me to distrust my body,
that companion to whom I was tied. I hadn't felt shame when I saw the

blood, just as I wasn't ashamed when my knee got hurt or my nose was bleeding. The shame transformed that blood into humiliation. Humiliation about which I couldn't even complain. Monthly humiliation, on a fixed schedule.

◈

I thought with envy about [the nude statue of Diana I had seen at the Jockey Club and about] Diana's thighs. Oh how I wished I were made of marble! Marble doesn't get stained with blood. . . . Who would ever have made a statue of Diana with her thighs defiled by blood? I thought that blood killed beauty. That it was killing my beauty. That I would rather not ever have been born.

I soon remembered with horror the large pieces of cotton material soaked in blood that, by chance, I had seen in a wash basin at the time my younger sister was born. I wondered if this blood had any relation to the blood that made its appearance every month. I despaired of the idea of that punishment as a monthly reminder that mine was a bloody destiny. . . . Slavery. An affront. Impossible to accept. Unthinkable. An unjust and dreadful sentence.

◈

It seemed to me that I wouldn't be able to tolerate life on those days when that blood arrived and that I would spend the rest of the month anguishing away, waiting for the next time. . . . I suffered so much that my suffering dissolved—like a cake of soap that is used over and over—by just wearing away. The third time the blood came, it seemed almost natural. But the feeling of rebellion and humiliation or of repudiation persisted, like the rumble of thunder in the distance, thunder that announced an imminent storm. What was I repudiating? The condemnation to silence for something people considered shameful, that had nothing to do with my own will, but was imposed on me by nature.

◈

Well, I wouldn't give in. With blood or without it, I would wash with cold water. I would climb the trapeze, bloody or not. And no power in the world would force me to have children. Babies that come out of the belly button. Pity not to be a chicken. (A,1:143–51)

Adolescence

An emerging beauty, Victoria now began a new life—of boys and dances, and rebellion. There is a shift in her style as she records her life as an adolescent. It is much more mature and complex and indeed is the style of the sixty-two-year-old woman who wrote it.

> My first communion, when I was twelve, didn't leave me with any pro-found memories. . . . My sister and I were prepared for it in the Church of San Juan. We had to recite the catechism to a French priest and we confessed to him in French. . . . I didn't like confession. It seemed repugnant to me, intrusive and indecent. I did it reluctantly because I was made to do it. I didn't enter into the spirit of that sacrament, either because they didn't know how to communicate the spirit of the ritual, or because I wasn't mature enough to understand it.
>
> As almost always happens in ceremonies, the material aspect of the event took on an importance of its own. The long white dress, the veil, the white missal, the new mother-of-pearl rosary, none of these whitened my soul (if color can be an attribute of one's soul). My soul was rather a rainbow that morning, in the Church of San Juan, with the altar full of light; I was think-ing of how beautiful my dress was and that I would only wear it once in my whole life. (A,2:41–42)

FAMILY RESTRICTIONS

> My father was always afraid that we would break our necks. For a while, for example, I rode a bicycle. But a doctor advised my father that bicycling wasn't good for young ladies. The bicycle disappeared. I used to go horse-back riding with my father. I had two ponies, Mosquito and The Bay. We used to ride as far as Martínez along the avenue of tipas trees that runs par-allel to the railroad tracks. I wore a blue riding outfit with a skirt and I rode as women do, on a saddle with a horn. The long skirt was already a great satisfaction in itself. Not to mention riding with my father. But that happiness didn't last long. My father thought that I was too daring or else he got tired of riding with me. On the ranch he wouldn't let me even ride the tamest pony. He was afraid I'd break a leg, or my head, the way I'd bro-ken my arm.
>
> We didn't have dogs. Beauty, a dog of my childhood, wasn't mine; he was a guard dog. My father thought we might catch some kind of disease from

the dog. We drank filtered water, or mineral water, or boiled milk. We never ate raw vegetables unless we knew where they came from. In Europe, when we arrived at some hotel, my mother would disinfect the toilets, the wash-basin, the bidet, and the bathtub before she would let us use them. Little did it matter that the hotel might be first class, as it was. Her standards for our cleanliness and hygiene always exceeded those of the hotel. On our first and second voyage to Europe we sailed with two cows and various chickens. And sheets. (A,2:21–23)

This overprotectiveness eventually led to other restrictions on Victoria. Years later Victoria told about how her mother acted as a censor when her father showed movies for the family at home.

If there were love scenes with kissing, my mother got up in the dark-ness of the hall—when you couldn't hear a sound except for the projector—cutting off our view. We protested without moving her. Since she wasn't able to guess how long the amorous passages would last—it was a silent movie and by covering up the figures she also covered up the words below—her precautionary shadow remained on the screen longer than necessary, some-times making us lose the thread of the story. (VW:45)

And there developed another, more serious, kind of censorship.

I was a good reader with a voracious, omnivorous appetite. The bad thing about this was that I wasn't able to just go to a bookstore to buy any book that interested me the way Ricardo Güiraldes could. There were a tremen-dous number of books on the family index. Some books were prohibited for incomprehensible reasons, since they had nothing to do with passionate romance (a forbidden subject unless . . . it dealt with a respectable kind of love that ended in marriage). An example of this censorship with no ap-parent motive was the sequestering of my copy of *De Profundis,* by Oscar Wilde, that my mother found under my pillow in the Hotel Majestic in Paris. I was nineteen. Of course there was a big scene when I declared that I wouldn't go on living this way and that I was ready to throw myself out the window. My mother took no notice of the threat, she didn't return the book, and she sailed out of my room saying that I was lacking in self-control. Right away I gave her plenty of reason to think so by throwing all my stockings out the window. It was a symbolic act, much heralded by the chauffeurs on the street below. (A,2:60–61)

I lived under an eminently patriarchal system of life, with all of the advantages and disadvantages that a patriarch imposes. Its disadvantages made me feel that I was the victim. I think I felt these disadvantages much more than any of our numerous servants who never seemed to imagine or need any other kind of existence. Or, if they did, they imagined it only very slightly and vaguely. The same was not true for me. I imagined it with all the intensity and rebellion of a prisoner, conscious of the walls that were cutting me off from other parts of society. I felt that I was a capable young person who wasn't able to take advantage of her talents nor to have an adequate education that would help her to develop fully. A person senses this intuitively every day. (A,2:16)

In those years I didn't go to dances and I was content just to see my mother dressed up for a dance in some Paris gown. As I say this I realize that I'm not telling the whole truth. I did more than just observe my mother. She had a very large closet, like a little room. And there, whenever the coast was clear, I would try on her dresses. I even dared to sneak out of my hiding place and have a look at myself in the mirror.

⁂

In grand houses such as my parents', people used to invite young girls to come for tea. They served little sandwiches and meringues with whipped cream and we girls would dance. Boys weren't invited. Such mixing wasn't the custom. Or if it was allowed, on rare occasions, it was only because some brother or boy cousin was already in the house and they felt he should be included.

We had dancing lessons at Mr. Forster's house. He, smelling of perfumed powder, dressed in a tailcoat at three in the afternoon and, wearing white gloves at any time of day, taught us to dance the waltz, the polka, the tarantella, the Washington Post . . . the mazurka. Everything except the tango, naturally. He taught us to curtsy gracefully without falling over. I was one of his best students. . . .

My first serious dance was a big event for me. It seemed to me that it was going to change my life because my "coming out" would give me an independence that I certainly didn't have at that time. . . . Until my first dance, I'd never had a chance to talk with boys aside from my numerous cousins who didn't count—except for C. . . . Because we were a family of girls, we didn't have brothers to bring friends home. To talk over the telephone to a boy, to write letters to a young man, to invite some boy who wasn't part of the family to come to the house, was not done, was not allowed.

When I was seventeen, as a concession to the modern ideas of those days, I was permitted to play golf at Mar del Plata with boys who were the sons of people my parents knew. We played as a foursome. From the golf house (more of a hut, really), our mothers used to follow us with binoculars. There were no trees on the course and only in a hollow by the sea did the players momentarily disappear from view. They disappeared four at a time with four caddies, never in pairs. Only by chloroforming six other people could a couple have managed to be alone in that hollow. As far as I know, no one even tried it.

We weren't permitted to play golf with the same person twice in succession. At dances, we were never allowed to dance several dances in a row with the same boy (a crucial necessity if the boy was serious). The only exception to this was the evening before announcing one's engagement. The continual change of partners annoyed me, for at dances, as in everything, I had decided preferences. My parents often scolded me, threatened to take away my golfing privileges, or took me home early just because, seated on a chair, with my partner seated on another chair, surrounded by fifty onlookers, I had stayed there talking with him through two whole dances. My behavior was considered quite improper.

All these prohibitions and limitations were creating a state of rebellion in me and it just kept getting worse. But the latent rebellion really had emerged before my presentation to society. It had started in my adolescence. (A,2:30–34)

INFATUATION[6]

One afternoon during Carnival, Victoria, who was then about fourteen, was out in front of her house in San Isidro. She had already taken off her devil's costume and, following the local custom, was throwing balloons filled with water at other merrymakers. She noticed a boy galloping by on his horse and was immediately attracted by his face, his blue eyes. He rode by again and again. Victoria felt surprise as it dawned on her that he kept returning because of her. Never before had she had this kind of attention from a boy. "He looked at me. He's seen me. An incredible, but evident, thing: I existed for him" (A,1:158).

Victoria threw a water bomb at him and he shouted back, "It didn't hit me." She kept repeating those words. She was enraptured, infatuated. She awoke the next morning and sensed that the rhythm of her life had changed. She wondered if he'd come back, and if he did, if it would be just to catch a glimpse of her. He came back.

Victoria learned through the servants that he was a distant cousin who lived only a few blocks away. He was older than Victoria and had what she saw as an air of indisputable superiority. She referred to him in her memoirs only as L. G. F.

From then on L. G. F. rode by every day. The two only looked at one another—without greeting, without even smiling. When fall came and Victoria realized that she would have to return to Buenos Aires, she was filled with anguish. She couldn't imagine afternoons without waiting for L. G. F. and she wondered if he knew where she lived in Buenos Aires and if she would ever see him again.

When L. G. F. did find her again, Victoria treated his return as a declaration of love. Every afternoon about five-thirty there L. G. F. would be, outside Victoria's house with its twenty-four balconies. The servants were in on Victoria's secret and seemed to take her side; her aunts and uncles were another matter. Soon Victoria began to think of L. G. F. and herself as victims of a much too careful vigilance. But this didn't stop the two from seeing each other, though seeing was all they could do.

One afternoon L. G. F. left three tea roses on one of the lower balconies. Victoria took off her shoes so she wouldn't make any noise and went down to retrieve the roses. She raced back to a higher balcony, and, holding them up to her face, showed them to L. G. F. Later, after she had dried them, she put them in her missal—her strong box. The next day she threw a small bouquet of violets to L. G. F. He picked them up, kissed them, and, when nobody was looking, blew a kiss. Victoria blew one back.

On Sundays when the family went to mass at Las Catalinas, L. G. F. was there, alone, waiting for Victoria. Sometimes their eyes met, but that was all. Victoria confessed that she fervently prayed in church, and before she went to sleep, that L. G. F. would love her as much as she loved him. She had complete confidence that God would give her His approval and support, and she thought of the Holy Trinity as her confidants.

When someone gave Victoria a postcard L. G. F. had sent him, Victoria hid it in her bedroom and brought it out at night to kiss it. She was thrilled to possess a card chosen, bought, and paid for by L. G. F. and with a stamp licked by his own tongue and put on by him, addressed by his own hand.

From the roof terrace of her aunts' house, Victoria could see the balconies of L. G. F.'s house. The terrace and the balcony became their secret meeting place where they waved white handkerchiefs to one another over the rooftops of Buenos Aires. One day a neighbor caught L. G. F. waving, got out his binoculars, and discovered Victoria on the receiving end of the fluttering handkerchief. The next time Victoria tried to go up to the roof, she found the door locked tight.

Victoria was quite convinced that the grown-ups in her family could never understand what L. G. F. meant to her and that only God could comprehend her happiness, a happiness that "radiated out in circles like the ones made by a stone thrown into a pond." It was a happiness, she writes, that "communicated to everything around me—the designs on the iron railings of the balcony, the sounds of the bells at the Catalinas church, the smell of yellow roses, the incense in church on Sundays . . . a happiness that invaded all dominions, the city, the country, the seasons, reading, music, heroes, saints, my prayers, my dreams" (A,1:173–74).

When spring came Victoria despaired because she and her family would be going to her grandparents' ranch in Pergamino—far, far away—for four interminable weeks. She was afraid L. G. F. would think she had forgotten him and would grow tired of waiting for her and never come back. L. G. F. appeared outside her house at six-thirty on the morning Victoria was to leave. With all her family around her, the farewell was brief: an opening and closing of the balcony, two hands that, from a distance, were joined together in the same farewell.

Victoria later acknowledged that if it hadn't been for reading and her growing pleasure in writing letters, that month away from Buenos Aires would have been one of tremendous emptiness. She began to realize that she liked to write just for the sake of writing and that it was a great release for her—a good way to confront feelings of injustice, loneliness, and boredom.

And then, experiencing one of the swift changes that come in adolescence, Victoria one morning awoke and it dawned on her that L. G. F. no longer interested her.

Other faces had taken his place on the screen of my imagination. Besides, I considered him too young; I was no longer excited by men who weren't a good bit older than I was. . . . Sometime between the time I was fifteen and twenty years old, the notion that only older men could interest me and understand me . . . began to dominate my thoughts. But I worried that such older men wouldn't notice me, or that I wouldn't be pleasing to them. My faith in my powers to conquer, that had been born with L. G. F., suffered a long eclipse. Years. (A,2:32,49)

When I passed L. G. F. at my first dance and felt completely indifferent to him, I didn't take it as a *warning*. It didn't occur to me that I had created L. G. F. in the image of my dreams, ignoring everything about the real person. It didn't occur to me that I had now obliterated that image the same way I had given it life. It didn't occur to me that I could repeat this offense. It didn't occur to me that, as I got older, a similar invention could have its repercussions, on both the inventor and the person invented. It did occur to me, on the contrary, that I had changed a great deal, a mistaken belief, for I went right on weaving a whole web of dreams around any male face that attracted me, and attributing to the bearer of that face superior qualities, virtues, gifts which he didn't possess. Or else I just interpreted the person as I wished, quite independently of any contradictory evidence. This infantile habit of mine continued, and was abetted by the enforced and fleeting superficiality of my relations with the opposite sex. (A,2:34)

The truth was that I idolized beautiful faces. I only learned years later that a face that was perfect physically could change into something hateful or simply boring when it was unmasked. But I was enjoying the webs I was spinning with my own imagination. When the beautiful face belonged to a woman, there was no danger. Feminine beauty had always fascinated me, but lesbianism had been an unknown temptation, an unknown territory for me. Man was my province. The danger came in imagining that I was really in love when, like a stupid spider, I was becoming trapped in a web of my own making. By imagining that I was in love, I could make a terrible mistake and be punished by a penalty harsher than death. As I saw it, marriage was a living death given the customs of those days. (A,2:39)

DOUBT AND CONFUSION

When Victoria was sixteen she began a correspondence with Delfina Bunge, a young friend in Buenos Aires who passed Victoria's family's scrutiny because she came from "a good family."[7] Delfina was twenty-five, intelligent, sensitive, and charming, and like Victoria, she loved to discuss literature. To add to her appeal, she was a poet and had a boyfriend, Manuel Gálvez, whom she later married, and who was a writer. Although Delfina was a practicing, believing Catholic and Victoria considered herself to be drifting away from the church, this didn't seem to create any problems. Victoria reported that she talked with Delfina freely about her doubts and lack of faith.

Here at last, was someone with whom Victoria felt free to share her innermost thoughts. Victoria considered her letters to Delfina to be significant because they revealed the degree to which she suffered as an adolescent and how much she was already troubled by the role women played in society and by the inferior quality of their education.

Victoria's first letter to Delfina had a pleading tone; it was appealing but rather childish. Years later, Victoria analyzed her "Do you want to be my friend?" as the adolescent equivalent of the early "Do you want to play with me?"

> BUENOS AIRES, 1906

Pardon me for bothering you. You must have better things to do. All I ask from you is a little friendship in exchange for the admiration and tenderness I feel for you. . . . I entreat you. You are happy, people like you, they understand you. . . . Moral isolation is painful. You don't know that terrible sensation of loneliness (surrounded by affection, I acknowledge). One suffers too much because the need to be understood is so great.

. . . A little friendship for me, Delfina. I am sixteen and at that age you need to confide in someone—if not the heart will burst. Do you want to be my friend? Do you want to listen to me? Answer me frankly. . . . If you find me horrifying, tell me so. I won't hide the fact that this would be painful. But I couldn't put up with the idea that I would be a burden to you. If I seem worthy of reading something of yours, I would be overjoyed. I am waiting for your letter. Really, can I let myself believe Delfina is my friend?

Delfina wrote back to Victoria with a positive, welcoming letter. Their correspondence was off and flying and Victoria was overjoyed. Here, as the following excerpts show, was a place for Victoria to express her confused ideas about love, and a way to articulate her apprehensions about trying to combine an intellectual life with marriage.

> BUENOS AIRES, 1906

You can't imagine the happiness your letter gave me, your long letter. I've read it three times. As usual, you are right. You are sensible and I am crazy. . . . It surprises me that an angel could like a devil, as much as that a devil could like an angel.

. . . What you say is right. I'm not content when just four or five people think the way I do, feel the way I do. I need understanding on a global scale. . . . You say that I suffer because I am hungering to love someone. Yes. But I have sworn that I will have only one great love: art. Go ahead and laugh. Art won't always be enough for me and I know it. The need to love someone is torturing me.

BUENOS AIRES, SEPTEMBER 14, 1907

Yes, you are right. When you're sixteen years old or seventeen, we love "love" in a crazy way. But despite all our struggles, all our efforts, despite realizing that what we feel is a love of love, nothing more, we end up falling in love with someone, whether he's half-blind or bow-legged. . . . We adorn that somebody with all the qualities we have (or wish we had). . . . We discover that we have completely invented him. . . . I have no idea of looking for a boyfriend, the way everyone else does. If someone extraordinary doesn't come along, I'd rather be an old maid. The longer I live the surer I am that I won't find anyone who is capable of understanding me. I'll stick with my books. For the moment.

BUENOS AIRES, SEPTEMBER 30, 1907

When I think that a person only lives once, that a person is only young once! Every minute that goes by without love, without a divine love, is like a century of wasted existence.

I have seen some ironic, intelligent eyes. I like them. Now, be careful! It's possible I've made up that look all by myself and that the eyes they belong to don't really have that look. I don't have any confidence in my imagination. Anyway, it's dangerous to look deep into those eyes. I've always adored beautiful eyes.

BUENOS AIRES,, DECEMBER 30, 1907

You ask me if I believe in the stars, in eyes, in dreams. But Delfina, I don't believe in anything else.

. . . to be loved and to be understood completely are one and the same thing for me. Love that isn't accompanied by a perfect harmony of ideas and sensitivities is not the love I want. The day when I don't believe in that love, I'll die of desperation. That love has to exist because I believe in it.

BUENOS AIRES, JANUARY 29, 1908

Literary ambitions? Of course I have them! If you knew, my dear, all that I would like to achieve, the writers I would like to equal!

But I won't succeed in doing anything with the novel. . . . I'd never be able to create a character. . . . All the characters would be "I" in disguise. Totally intolerable.

CHAPTER TWO ❧ FIRST LOVES

In 1908 Victoria's letters to Delfina introduced Bernardo de Estrada (Monaco), the young man she eventually married, to whom she gave the fictitious name Jerome. Her letters suggested why she was attracted to him, as well as why she had doubts about marrying him.[1]

Jerome

BUENOS AIRES, APRIL 2, 1908

I want to tell you how I met that person. Let's just call him Jerome. I suggest this name because he's always talking about Jerome Coignard (Anatole France). Jerome is the prototype of the skeptic, he's ironic.

Back in April of 1906 . . . I had the idea of playing tennis at my grandfather's house in San Isidro. I kept after my mother to take us. I was so happy when we got on the train to go there that I began to sing, but Mother made me be quiet. Before the train left who should pass by but Jerome, whom I'd never before seen up close. He walked by with that disdainful air he has when he knows people are looking at him. His head is beautiful, but—I thought—Why put up with this? Who does he think he is?

We arrived at my grandfather's estate and started to play tennis. About three-thirty, right in the middle of a game, we saw a carriage pull up. "What a nuisance!" we said in chorus. It turned out to be Jerome with a friend. They sat down on a bench near the court and we went on with our game; I didn't show the least interest in them (which, of course, was just a pretense).

When we finished we went over and sat down under the trees. . . . Someone introduced me to Jerome. I gave him my left hand because my racquet was in the other hand. We talked a little. He wasn't being easy on anyone that afternoon. It was his own way of flirting. He came out with charming, witty remarks, but always with a sarcastic edge.

I remember everything: the cloudless sky, the golden trees, the brick house, the smell of autumn. We talked about Heredia's sonnets. Jerome made a joking allusion to girls who wrote poetry in French and chose the sonnet for their maiden voyage. We talked about reciting poetry. He made fun of girls who recited and put them in a category with clever monkeys. In general, he was right. But to put me in the company of clever monkeys was an insult I couldn't let pass without wanting to throttle him. . . . His narcissistic air infuriated me. "I'll make you pay for your contempt, you and your pompous erudition, and your looking down your nose at me. You'll learn how clever monkeys are. Foul mouthed ignoramus, poisonous character."

When I got home I wrote in my diary that I intended to make friends with Jerome, but first I needed to get him mad, for, if I couldn't inspire a little passion, at least I'd get his attention that way. I liked him and yet I didn't like him. He interested me and yet he irritated me. But I found him physically splendid (his face).

At my first dance he wasn't there. At my second I saw him from a distance. He didn't even come over to say hello. . . . At the third dance he came over and asked me if I'd do him the honor of conversing with him. He supposed that his ceremonious tone would annoy me because anyone could plainly see that the honor was mine. With an equal desire to irritate him, I told him that he should come back later. He did come back (I was afraid he wouldn't).

We talked for the first time, tête-à-tête. Alternately admiring and facetious, he would compliment me and then say something disagreeable that nullified his words of praise. I did the same thing. . . . And so, in this way, from dance to dance, that amorous friendship (in my case) was born.

BUENOS AIRES, APRIL 14, 1908

You ask me if he's serious. What do I know? I'm not sure of anything, least of all myself.

BUENOS AIRES, MAY 1908

I heard that Jerome said that writing poetry was a charming trick, that I was like those little dogs that stand on their hind legs. I don't like it . . . I don't like it one bit. It's all over. He's no longer the person of my dreams.

Fifteen days ago I told myself: Jerome is an invention of mine. I've invented him. He's a fake.

. . . Now that I can think straight, I realize that Jerome will never take my ambitions seriously.

BUENOS AIRES, JUNE 1908

I'd like to go to Europe. To get away from here. I have to get away. I have to. To anywhere. Or I'll die. Nobody, nobody. I am going through a spell of Purgatory.

BUENOS AIRES, JULY 5, 1908

It seems as if I'm standing on the edge of a cliff and the least bit of wind will make me lose my balance and I'll fall over.

Jerome's sterile ambitions sour him. He doesn't have any clear idea of what he wants and he lacks the courage to set any plan in motion. Ridicule horrifies him. He suffers from excessive self-esteem. He can never forget himself. But you'd have to show him his faults without his realizing that you're doing it.

During the time that she was first writing to Delfina, Victoria also had as a close friend the French actress Marguerite Moreno, who in 1905 began coaching Victoria in recitation. As their relationship developed, the sophisticated actress became a trusted confidant who had a strong influence on the young and troubled Victoria.

By 1908, even though it was four years before Victoria would marry Jerome, she had already begun to entertain thoughts of marriage. Moreno countered with sensible arguments designed to make Victoria consider the consequences before she took such a precipitous step. Victoria reported this to Delfina.

BUENOS AIRES, JULY 7, 1908

I'm having gloomy thoughts. And what Marguerite was telling me today doesn't clear things up for me. "My Hedgehog" (that's what she calls me) "you are letting yourself be carried away by a feeling that is only amorous pity. Have you any idea what that man is like? Are you sure he will understand you? Let us admit, let us suppose, that he is intelligent. Do you know what kind of an intelligence he has? Are you sure, little one, that two years from now you won't have developed in new directions? And if you evolve, which seems inevitable to me, are you sure you will find some echo in him? A woman like you ought not to become engaged lightly. How much remorse you would have later! Listen to me carefully, my dear. . . . You are a woman who is very capable of judging her husband and of making him aware that you're judging him. Men don't like that. Your intelligence is much more active than his."

The next day Victoria wrote to Delfina reflecting on Moreno's warning and on her own fear of succumbing to a lifetime of dull married domesticity that would stunt both her mind and her personality. She felt herself bursting with intelligence and concluded, with exuberant determination, that she had the courage to give up marriage for the life of the mind.

BUENOS AIRES, JULY 8, 1908

Never, never in my life will I be able to resign myself to suppressing my own personality. I understand that a woman should make this sacrifice for love. But not me. I can't. . . . I'm not a fragile plant that wants to feel protected under the shade of some vigorous tree. I have a lot of love inside me, but I am also intoxicated with freedom and intellectual strength.[2]

BUENOS AIRES, JULY 23, 1908

I want to read Schopenhauer, Nietzsche, Renan, Voltaire, etc. I want to read everything. How? (There are certain books they won't let me read.)

Today I saw Jerome in the street. I also saw H. and C. B. Always in the street. I receive in the street. My living room is the street. But, of course, I don't talk with anyone.

BUENOS AIRES, AUGUST 1, 1908

Jerome came to Mass. He sent me a jasmine with a friend and asked me to wear it. If I put it on that would mean that I loved him. I didn't put it on. He wants me to show my hand first.

BUENOS AIRES, AUGUST 26, 1908

The other day I was looking at some photos of Maud Allan dancing "Springtime" of Grieg and "Salome" of Strauss. She is twenty years old and they say she has a perfect body. From what I can see, that's true. She is almost nude in the pictures. A chaste nudity because of its very beauty. A prudish relative of mine stopped me cold: "How can you look at that? Quick, turn the page. It's indecent." I don't believe in the indecency of nudity. Nor in the indecency of writing what one feels.

BUENOS AIRES, SEPTEMBER 26, 1908

The fictitious life I live weighs on me. That life invented by men's foolishness. What a travesty! I wasn't born for that! I'm better than that. Don't laugh at me. I'm talking about my isolation.

Tonight I'm going to a dance. It wouldn't surprise or shock me if people look at me with wonder, malevolence, curiosity, lust, aversion, or sympathy. What does it matter to me!

BUENOS AIRES, SEPTEMBER 27, 1908

Last night I saw Jerome. I talked with him. Why deceive myself? I like him. Does he like me? He pretends to. But is it possible to be suspicious and jealous to that extreme? He reproaches me—even keeping his eye on the doors and windows; it occurs to him that I'm waiting for someone else. This is madness. He says I flirt with X., Y., and Z. As a matter of fact, with all the letters of the alphabet. He says that whenever he sees me surrounded by admirers he feels tremendous bitterness.

BUENOS AIRES, OCTOBER 21, 1908

As to marriage and the role of women, . . . things are beyond belief. Nobody minds if the man goes on living his bachelor's life after he's married. . . . The woman has to put up with this without complaining. But I think marriage should be a pact that bears the same obligations, the same freedoms for both people. If the man abandons the woman, it's stupid for the woman to just sit in a chair, waiting for him. Do I shock you?

. . . Man is a beast who abuses his freedom and the legal power that social prejudices give him. Prejudices of which the woman is the victim. Ah! Delfina, it terrifies me to think that I could forget all this if I fell in love with someone and let myself be put in chains.

(My mother told me that my grandmother, or great grandmother, had a gold bracelet inscribed with the words "chained and happy." I said to my mother, "But was she crazy?")

There are two contrary, irreconcilable forces in me: my head and my heart. My heart loves, is gullible, trusting, tender. My head doubts, rebels, disdains, denies.

. . . The fact is that the pompous profanations that are imposed on me in the name of religion only drive me further away from Catholicism. This debasing of the doctrine of Jesus seems criminal to me. Everything is sold in the temples. Water from Lourdes along with the rest. A woman who just died left an enormous amount of money so they'll say mass after mass for the repose of her soul. I wouldn't want to pay money like that for the salvation of my soul. The poor devils who die without any ceremonies or any masses are left to be roasted on the grills of Hell. Isn't that right?

Catholicism, as I see it practiced, seems to me narrow, limited, irritating, empty, hypocritical. I can't respect it.

On the outside I do more or less what everyone does, for my mother's sake. If I didn't, it would be a catastrophe for her. But that deception can't last. It weighs too much on me.

PARIS, DECEMBER 30, 1908

Today I long for the sun, for the Argentine sky. For the first time I understand that we're tied to the land where we're born. I love [Argentina].

When I think about the garden in San Isidro, about its flowers (they're blossoming this month), what a feeling of homesickness! Why bother traveling if you already have within yourself all the beauty in the world?

I like Paris. But I'm writing you to talk about my nostalgia for Buenos Aires. . . . Have you seen Jerome? Do you have any news of him?

PARIS, JANUARY 10, 1909

I'm taking courses in literature and philosophy at the College of France and the Sorbonne (nobody makes me). . . . The life I live here is almost ideal. But thinking about Jerome ruins my happiness. When I realize that it is summer there, that the garden is full of flowers, that there are peaches and blue sky, I feel wretched, exiled. Here the sky is always gray. And when it isn't gray, I feel sad because the day is beautiful. What sense does a life without love make after you're eighteen?

PARIS, APRIL, 1, 1909

I'm afraid that what attracts me about Jerome might also blind me. What I know of him is what it pleases me to know . . . not the truth. I like the beauty of his eyes better than the things he says.

At times I understand what's going on with this love. But the "I" that has fallen in love is impetuous and young. The "I" that reasons is afraid and just lets itself be dragged along.

PARIS, SEPTEMBER 20, 1909

I see myself and feel too human not to madly detest myself. I have all the weaknesses, all the miseries and riches of that perverse, lying, stupid, false humanity that exasperates me.

PARIS, NOVEMBER 19, 1909

. . . I couldn't help but laugh when your letter arrived and you advised me to work. [The writer] Carlos Reyles has just preached the same thing to me—only his words were harsher.

He wrote me that if I didn't work seriously, I, a new kind of Cleopatra, would end up doing something stupid that would cost me dearly: getting married. That I shouldn't even consider marriage until I'm twenty-five.

But what to work on? I work in my own way, and because I want to. But my parents won't let me pursue the work that is closest to my heart: the theater.

PARIS, MARCH 2, 1910

I have an incurable disease, and it can't be attributed to any external cause: an absolute desperation. I'm young, people admire me, men fall in love with me, I'm intelligent, healthy, and full of life. I live in the lap of luxury, I can aspire to almost anything, my strong will makes all things possible (except freedom . . . I want to dedicate myself to the theater) and in spite of all this, I am filled with a deep inner despair.

PARIS, MARCH 9, 1910

Today Hauvette wound up his course on *The Divine Comedy.* What a shame! It seems to me that some of Dante's verses were written just for me. Dante's soul is a kindred spirit of my soul. I feel full of talent, of intelligence, of love that I would like to communicate. I was born to do great things that I'll never do, because of an excess of everything.

. . . I don't know where to escape. And when I think I'm drowning in those vague ambitions, in that surplus of life and talent that overwhelms me because I don't use it, the only thing that I can do is complain in a letter, in an abominable style, of the wretchedness of the society into which I was born.

BIARRITZ, APRIL 24, 1910

. . . Am I already addressing Mme. Manolo Gálvez? You'll always be Delfina Bunge to me. I've been thinking about you a lot and I'm sorry not to be in Buenos Aires. Did you get married? This saddens me; excuse me. Marriage seems so frightening to me!

SAN ISIDRO, SUNDAY, 1912

I was going to write you to announce my engagement to Jerome. . . . Try to come soon, my dear. I'm not proposing that I go see you because I still don't go out alone. Someone always has to go with me and it's an exasperating situation.

Years later, in her autobiography, Victoria tried to recreate her state of mind as she was making the big decision to marry Jerome.

. . . Of the young men with whom I kept company when I was young (and let's not forget that it was an extremely limited keeping of company), the one who most attracted me, because he was the most intelligent and handsome, was Jerome. We only saw each other at dances and at the hippodrome on the occasion of the bishop's death or at the Ice Palace which was all the fashion then. When my sister Clara died in 1911, attendance at the dances, the races, the Ice Palace all ceased. However, one day [while the family was still in mourning], a relative, who was allowed to come to the house, brought Jerome, so he could pay a visit. This already was a step that com-

promised a young woman in a certain respect, given the thinking and prejudices of those times in general and my family in particular (the house of
Bernarda Alba).

The two young men presented themselves one afternoon. After Jerome
came visiting three or four times, my father called me into his study (these
audiences were never pleasant) and asked me *what I intended to do.* Get married or what? To go on like this, receiving visits from this young man did not
look right. . . . My father's paternal attitude had the effect of pushing me toward a decision that I might not have made if I had felt free . . . that is, if I
had been able to talk with Jerome and meet with him and other friends without worrying that it would have consequences. So I decided to become
engaged. Otherwise I wouldn't be allowed to see Jerome any more. It was
the only way out of the cage I was in. The worst way. . . . I resigned myself
to create another worse jail, although at that moment I didn't calculate
the consequences that marriage would bring.

Of course, I believed I was in love with Jerome. All the same, our different
ways of looking at life and reacting to things made me uneasy. Jerome was
of a suspicious nature and out of the blue would accuse me of something I'd
never do.

One day Jerome asked me if a man had ever kissed me. I realized from
his look and tone of voice that this question was a touchstone for him. . . .
In a second I thought: And what right do you have to reproach me for this?
Haven't you known and kissed other women? And what women they will
have been! The one kiss I might have been able to confess, the only one, was
a spontaneous, fleeting kiss; . . . passionate, but almost infantile, given its innocence. . . . I answered him like a person defending herself: "No." "Are you
sure"? "No."

That, I believe, is where my big mistake began. I should have answered:
"Yes. Someone kissed me once. And what about it? What collection of vir-
ginities do you intend to bring to our marriage? Have I asked for an account
of your actions? Or for a numerical count of your lovers. Am I not a human
being just like you?" (A,2:167–71)

Marriage

In Buenos Aires, on the afternoon of November 8, 1912, Victoria was married
to Monaco Estrada, "Jerome." Victoria recalled her wedding in her memoirs.

The religious ceremony for my marriage took place in the house on Florida and Viamonte. Naturally my hair was arranged, my veil put in place, and I was assured that I was lovely (a routine matter) by Martín Soulés, the hairdresser who for years reigned supreme in Buenos Aires and whipped into shape the hair of both young and old of high society.

. . . As happens at wakes, first communions, etc., this ceremony is imbued with material details that denaturalize it, distract attention from it, and focus on superficialities. "Does the tulle fall properly? Put another pin here, Martín." "Yes, my lovely child." "Don't put those daisies that way. I'll look like one of those brides in the window of some cheap shop. Do you hear me, Martín?" "How could I not hear you! Give me time! What a child, Victoria!" (A,2:161)

Soon Victoria was descending the grand staircase on the arm of her grandfather Ocampo, who, once down, saw fit to adopt a slow military step, sending each leg forward and upward in a stylized goose step that threw Victoria off in every sense of the word. To make matters worse, the groom's suit reeked of moth balls, a smell that bothered Victoria as it entered her sensitive nose and lingered in her memory for years to come.

In her brief account of her wedding, Victoria added only the noncommittal sentence: "On the fifteenth of December Monaco and I sailed together for Europe" (A,2:163).

A few weeks after my marriage M. and I were in Paris, at the Hotel Meurice on the Rue de Rivoli (first floor, facing the Tuilleries). On Sundays when we would go to the Bois and come across a couple embracing and kissing along one of the paths, I felt lonely. I wasn't happy enough nor in love enough not to envy the woman. Settled into a mediocre happiness (the kind I might feel in a good hotel where nothing belonged to me), I didn't even believe in happiness. I hadn't articulated this conclusion in precise terms; perhaps because I didn't consent to the idea. But with my consent or without it, my heart was footloose. . . .

I didn't dislike M. yet. . . . But his character, his conventional ideas, his prejudices, his reactions all gave me an uneasy feeling. His suspicion and his jealousy bothered me too. . . .

M.'s jealousy was mostly a matter of self-love. We were as little made for each other as a bird and a fish (with no possibility of living in the same environment). Perhaps I would have felt pity for sensual jealousy, but jealousy arising from self-love annoyed me and provoked reactions in me that were as uncommendable as the ones that had aroused them. Despite everything, M. gave me free rein, treating me like a little lap-dog that occasionally gets obstinate and barks. Let's be perfectly clear: I had no calling for the role of lap-dog, and I didn't take long to show it. . . .

The new life we were living in Paris, with the freedom to go to performances that had been prohibited to me just two months earlier (plays, the ballet Russe, etc.) was diverting for me. During my earlier long stay in that city I adored, I had only been allowed to go to the classic matinee of the Comédie Francaise (Racine, Corneille, Molière). Now I was reading whatever appealed to me without stirring up any arguments. Seen, admired, flattered to the point of nausea by saleswomen from the great couturiers, sought after by the fashionable portrait artists (Boldini), I was "all bedazzled still," as Massenet's Manon sings. The secret, unconfessed premonition of disaster had not yet risen to the surface, but way down deep inside myself, I had a sense of uneasiness.

In February we went to Rome. We missed the morning train and had to leave on the night one. I don't know why I remember that unimportant detail. For the first time in my life I was late getting to the station. There was nothing irreparable about the incident, and yet it disquieted me. And so began that trip to Italy. We stayed at the Grand Hotel, the rendezvous of cosmopolitan Italian aristocracy (that dissolute society according to Fani, my faithful nursemaid, and now my Cerberus) . . . who welcomed us with open arms. (A,3:11–13)[3]

Our frivolous life of dances, concerts, museums, palaces, and ruins was spiced with fighting. . . . M. would accuse me of trying to attract attention. Do you know why they've asked us to the Colonna Ball? "No. Why"? "Because of you." I didn't understand that kind of reproach. But gradually these wounding outbursts began to harden my heart.

❧

The atmosphere was tense in Rome, just four months after my marriage, without it being my fault, and maybe not M.'s either. He went right on being what he had been: a handsome young man (I detested that beauty when I learned to decipher it), intelligent (if I compared him with the young men I usually saw), but with an intelligence that was disconnected from feeling. Touchy, tyrannical and weak, conventional, devoured by self-love . . . the sum total was that everything conspired so that I no longer loved him. Before I was married, I had the illusion of loving him. . . . I suspected that we didn't understand one another, but I thought I'd be able to change all that. What a stupid pretension! A few months of marriage and the scaffolding constructed by my imagination and my need to fall in love came tumbling down in ruins. Our love quickly shattered because M. wasn't able to hold me either with his heart, or with his intelligence or with the senses. He was an object of my own creation, an object that fell apart in my hands. If I'd had the freedom to know him better, before I'd gotten married, I never would have done it. This doesn't mean that my deception was physical. It was less a matter of the senses than a matter of tenderness. Physically I was so normal and so made for man that I couldn't have been frustrated by even the worst of lovers. When I would fall in love, as a girl (although I had no experience of the sexual act), I realized that men also excited me sexually. What I felt didn't depend on what my companion was able to reveal to me. I considered myself physically and intellectually developed and equal to him. (A,3:17–19)

Julian

In the first days of April, in Rome, four and a half months after Victoria and Monaco were married, Victoria met Julian Martínez (the J. of Victoria's autobiography). She didn't know anything about him except for some gossip about an affair, and that many people judged him severely, calling him a libertine.

Julian was her husband's cousin; it was Monaco who introduced Victoria to this man who would change her life so profoundly.

> The instant I saw J., at a distance, his presence overwhelmed me. He gave me a joking, tender look. (Later I discovered that his eyes often had that expression.) I looked at that look and that look looked at my mouth, as if my mouth were my eyes. My mouth, a prisoner of that look, began to tremble. I wasn't able to parry his look the way he might have parried mine. It lasted an entire century; a second. We shook hands. (A,3:19–20)

Victoria and Monaco went back to Paris. When Victoria learned that Julian had also returned, she persuaded a reluctant Monaco to invite Julian to accompany them to the ballet. Victoria admitted that she watched Nijinsky dancing "The Specter of the Rose" without really seeing it. As the three left the theater, the couple suggested that Julian come back to their place. Julian refused and Victoria thought to herself, "Some woman is waiting for him," and she felt devastated. She was hopelessly enveloped by a love that she admitted was absurd, a love that her infuriated reason tried to reject.

The newlyweds returned to Buenos Aires, months went by, and Victoria became absorbed in the complex business of settling into a new house. She believed that she had forgotten Julian. Then, quite by surprise, during a performance of "Parsifal" at the Colón Theater, Victoria caught a glimpse of Julian. Once again she felt "like tiny iron filings attracted to a magnet." She later recalled that great waves of Wagner's music carried her to their crest and broke on the very place where Julian was sitting.

Victoria and Julian soon met again at a dinner party. By chance she was seated directly across from him. She raised her eyes and saw herself in his eyes. His look overcame her and she felt faint. When Victoria returned to her senses she wondered with alarm if anyone had observed this explicit confession of love. From then on Victoria's problems multiplied.

M. became increasingly arbitrary and jealous and wouldn't tolerate my talking with other men if he imagined that for some reason they interested me. It only took the least insignificant thing to unleash his suspicions. If I smoked in front of people, if at some dance I spoke French with a cousin, my behavior was considered close to that of a slut. He even threatened once to lock me up in the house. . . .

To see J. after that was an impossibility. Better not to even say his name. M. had declared war on him. . . . M.'s tyrannical attitude only increased my aversion to him and put in relief the odious side of a marriage where all the rights were reserved for the man.

❧

One day M. received an anonymous letter which he never showed me; the writer mentioned my relationship with J. The effect of the letter was devastating. My relationship with J. was *nonexistent* at that moment . . . but I couldn't deny that I was thinking about him constantly. . . . I felt paralyzed by apprehension about my parents' reaction, though neither M.'s nor public opinion meant anything to me. The first thing M. would do, given his ways, would be to speak to my father (as if I were a minor). The fear of upsetting my mother and father put a tight rein on me.

❧

When I heard that M. had received a second anonymous letter, I decided to telephone J. Standing among the flowers in Chauvin's flower shop on Esmeralda Street, I called and quickly told him what had happened and added that *M. and I could no longer live in peace.* I also added that the anonymous letters which were poisoning the atmosphere were undoubtedly written by a jealous, poorly informed woman. Jealous of what, holy God! J. told me that he was desolate and that he couldn't imagine anyone doing such an infamous thing. I said: "Find her. *She's someone you know.*"

❦

The anonymous letters precipitated events. After my first call, I telephoned again (always from some shop and for a brief conversation). The letters kept on coming. . . . I was horribly jealous of the jealousy that I myself was inspiring. . . .

Soon I became accustomed to calling him—sometimes from Marguerite Moreno's house. We would talk for a short while. We would suggest books to one another. We read Colette, de Maupassant, Vigny. We would make dates to read them at the same time. "At ten tonight. Is that possible?" Separated by twenty blocks, I in my house, he in his, we would read. The next day we would comment on our reading. . . .

I was living, yearning, for those few minutes when our voices would answer each other. I was also living in the terror that those minimal conversations would be discovered and perhaps interrupted. Every night I went back home shaking for fear of bad news. Once we made a date to meet in a bookstore, just so we could see each other from a distance. We didn't even greet one another. . . .

Things were getting worse and worse with M. Separation would have been the only solution. But that was out of the question. He wouldn't accept such an idea and instead would brandish his weapon of talking to my father. Appearances counted a great deal to M. They were nothing to me. And his Catholicism was incomprehensible: there was no compassion or charity in it. We didn't talk to one another except when we were with other people.

Rebellion was growing in me. A year and some months had gone by since I had met J. in Rome. I had never conversed with him alone. Our dialogues were confined to the telephone. . . . "I'm only afraid on account of you. But if you're careful and take a taxi and meet me at the corner of Leandro Alem, near the Casa Rosada, it's almost impossible for anyone to follow you." . . .

So one afternoon, after a number of twists and turns, of going in through one shop door and out through another, like a criminal running away from the police, I reached the taxi at the agreed-on place. Sitting next to each other in that taxi we were no longer the same two people as on the telephone. Once again we had to overcome our mutual timidness. We stopped using the familiar form of address. Of course our voices were familiar to one another, but we ourselves were not. J. wanted to take my hand; I withdrew it brusquely. After a silent moment I said: "What a horror—this business of clandestine meetings. Nothing I feel is clandestine. Why am I condemned to this? If this is *the price* for our encounters, I'll learn to detest them. I refuse to accept this secretiveness. *If I accept it I would be betraying myself, do you understand?* But you, you're used to this kind of thing." "When it's you and I feel the way I do, I'm not used to things like this. Why do you say things like that, Victoria?" (A,3:26–31)

It bothered me a great deal to have to hide, to find myself sitting in a taxi next to an unknown man! Humiliation was consuming my pride. . . . The street was dark. J. had told the driver just to go on driving and the driver understood perfectly that we weren't going anywhere. This made me bristle. We had indirectly made him think that we were lovers or that we would be soon.

We were silent for a few minutes (centuries?). Suddenly, as if asking his pardon, I kissed J. without saying a word. We no longer had anything to say to one another. He put his arms around me and held me close. We spoke no words but felt bound to one another. The relief of physical contact. It invaded our beings, eliminating all the rest. Relief and happiness. . . .

When we separated, a half-hour later (a half-hour so short and so definitive), I knew nothing of the present, of the past, of the virtues, of the vices, of the character of that unknown man whose presence was flooding me with happiness. But I knew, this much I did know, that I was determined to lie without remorse just to sit next to him for a half-hour in a taxi, nothing more. A case of legitimate defense, I repeated to myself. Legitimate defense against a contemptible society to which I myself didn't belong, but to which my mother and father certainly did. (A,3:34–35)

Often when Victoria returned from one of her secret rendezvous with Julian, she would be greeted by a shaken Fani with the alarming news that Victoria had received an anonymous call warning her that she shouldn't take taxis, that she was being followed. Victoria began to suspect that her mother was using Fani to spy on her; she felt this intrusive surveillance as a persecution, but said not a word of her suspicions to either her mother or Fani—and she went right on meeting secretly with Julian whenever she had the chance.

One day J. arrived at our trysting place with good news; his family had gone to Córdoba for a few days so the house on Rodríquez Peña was empty. (He lived there with his mother, a brother and a married sister.) . . . We agreed that I would go to his house the following day, as soon as it began to get dark. Even after so many years I can still hear the echo of my footsteps as they approached that door on the street. It seemed to me that the whole universe heard their clatter. There were only a few people on the street, but I looked with suspicion at each one of them.

The door was partly open. I went in. J. was waiting for me ("Has anyone followed you?") and locked the door. He took my hand and led me over to the stairs. There were no lights on. "Come up. Careful! There's another step. This is the landing. Come in. This is my room." The fire in the fireplace flashed light and shadows on the walls.

⁓

That evening we spent an hour lying in bed. Our bodies understood one another. We had nothing to teach them. I doubt that other bodies have ever had greater understanding, greater pleasure in becoming intimate with one another and with more tenderness to lavish when their desire was satisfied and fading away. We desired each other far beyond desire, not only for those fleeting moments. Just to look at one another, to hold hands, to feel together the warmth of the fire, everything was happiness.

But the clock existed. It measured a different time from the one we were living in. "Don't let me go," I said as I stood in the doorway of his room. "Would you leave your parents for me? Would you be happy separated from them? You know that there's no other obstacle." I didn't answer. I fled like someone condemned to life. (A,3:38–39)

It was clear by this time that Victoria's marriage to Monaco was over, although it was years before they got a legal separation. The only problem for Victoria now was her parents. She said that she was tied to her mother and father by a canine faithfulness that seemed human in a dog and almost animal in a man.

Soon after this first sexual encounter, Julian rented an apartment for them

on Garay Street. Victoria remembers it as a sad, ugly place that smelled of
forage from a nearby stockyard, a smell that even after many years she could
still recall.

> Little by little I transformed those rooms and the place became attractive.
> I had the walls papered white. For the bedroom I chose a few pieces of an-
> tique furniture which I had J. buy. I rented a piano. The bad thing was
> that the sun never made its way to that apartment. But even if it had been
> a cave, I would have liked it. . . . Whenever the doorman would see me,
> he would immediately offer his services without being asked. This friend-
> liness, surely born of the succulent tips J. gave him, made him seem like
> an accomplice and it really bothered me. When J. arrived I would wrap
> my arms around him like a shipwrecked person does to a life preserver. Cry-
> ing, from humiliation or rage, I would say to him: "Isn't this life ever going
> to change? I can't stand this hide-and-seek any longer. I'm fed up with the
> role of an adulteress." (A,3:41)

Julian would have been happy to go away with Victoria, but he knew she
would have to make that decision for herself. The overwhelming question
was whether it would be possible for Victoria to leave her parents. Did she have
the courage to live with the consequences? Frantic conversations about their future didn't really solve their complex problems.

Then mutual jealousy entered their lives and further deteriorated their relationship. Victoria was intensely jealous of the women in Julian's past life, but
she considered it ridiculous for Julian to be jealous of any of the men in her life
because those men meant little to her. The fact is she couldn't imagine loving
anyone but J. Even years later she said that she never felt that kind of attraction,
that kind of passion, for any other man.

Jealousy punctuated their days and nights with accusations and quarrels. Julian began to feel inadequate and worried that the atmosphere of continual hiding and constant contention would gradually wear Victoria down. He began to
feel that the spark was going out of him and he worried about the effect on their
affair.

> . . . "I'm a dull man compared to the life and intelligence that radiates
> from you. You'll end up being tired of me, of these poor rooms, of these
> clandestine meetings that force you into a thousand subterfuges, of every-
> thing in this type of relationship that is repugnant to you. You're made for
> a different destiny. I can't offer you anything but love and tenderness. I re-

alize that the tenderness I give you is something you didn't have before, something you needed. But I also know that you need other things as well."

⁂

J. would say to me: "Ever since we started seeing each other I've never looked at another woman." But even if I could have enclosed him in an airtight crystal box, my jealousy wouldn't have been diminished. I was jealous of how other women had pleased him, or of the way these women had found pleasure in him. (A,3:49–50)

Victoria was now close to touching bottom. Her marriage was a disaster, she had moments of detesting her parents, her secret life with Julian had become increasingly stressful. Reflecting on her frenzied state, Victoria rebelled against the life she was leading and, in the process, let fly at Argentine men.

Argentine men, those primitive men, those authoritarian, jealous "own-ers" of women who generally divided women into two categories: respectable women—mothers, wives, sisters, etc.—and women who have no right to be respected, made for fly-by-night copulation, adulterous women, crazy vir-gins or absolute prostitutes. This second category, adulteresses, is where I be-longed. (A,3:60)

Difficult as it may have been, their life together went on. There were even some light moments, such as the time when they found a restaurant where they could be together in carefree anonymity.

. . . I had fun putting on an act for the waiter—a comedy about a happily married bourgeois couple. While he was serving us, I would talk to J. about our children, about how they looked like such-and-such person in the fam-ily, about their illnesses, about the cook and the nursemaid. J. would laugh his head off. But my words seemed perfectly normal to the astonished waiter and he didn't understand what could be causing all this hilarity. . . . After the waiter had gone away I would say to J.: "Deep down, you know, I envy couples who can really talk this way." I ridiculed them because I envied them.

Toward the end of spring, when the tipas were in bloom and the side-walks along the Ninth of July were covered in deep yellow tamarind leaves, . . . I thought I was pregnant. A gynecologist I'd gone to earlier had said:

"Nothing is the matter with you. Your menstrual pains are normal; they'll disappear as soon as you have a baby. You are made to have children." Those words, that diagnosis, kept coming back like a refrain.

J. couldn't believe it. In a state of panic, he would look at my extraordinarily flat stomach . . . as if he were waiting for some direct revelation. He covered it with kisses as if he could touch the baby, so it would have pity on us. I had the sensation of playing host to a body that was obeying its own laws without taking me into account in any way. A strange body, independent of me, which if it wanted to might play a nasty trick on me.

. . . I longed to have a child with J. (having a child with M. would have been repugnant), but under our circumstances it seemed to me absolutely impossible—for the child and for the parents. . . . J. and I deliberated over all possible solutions, including atrocious ones which I never seriously considered. But abortion never even crossed my mind. . . . Return to my husband for the child's sake? Inconceivable.

⁂

. . . I had a fixed idea, but I didn't communicate it to J.: suicide. Death and birth are solitary acts.

At dawn the next day, almost without having slept, I woke up damp with blood. I got up and, still in my night gown, I went onto the terrace off my room: Thank you, fate, I thought. (A,3:71–74)

Never before had I known the desire [that women have to immortalize the man they love with a child]. That deep longing of the heart had never expressed itself in me before I met J. I had been obsessed with birth control because I had never wanted to have a child with M. I thought I was incapable of wanting them. All that changed with J. (A,3:79)

J. and I never went out in "society" together, but I went to dances, and sometimes I would have a group of friends to my house. I especially liked to dance with good dancers like Ricardo Güiraldes and V. M. None of that provoked any conflicts. J. was generous with me, and besides, he knew perfectly well that men who showed me attention didn't matter one bit to me. He was the only man who counted for me. I never hid anything from him (and there wasn't anything to hide). (A,3:85)

But while J. might be generous on most occasions, it was quite a different matter when Victoria developed a friendship that hinted of love. Victoria was quick to realize that any invasion of the territory encompassed by their own passionate love undermined Julian's spirit and reason.

Soon another man appeared on the scene and put Victoria and Julian's love and liberal views to the test. Shortly after World War I a French aviator arrived in Buenos Aires in his well-cut uniform. This handsome war hero, "Z," was introduced to Victoria at a dance. Victoria was intrigued as, dancing with him, she listened to his stories about flying at night. Z. responded enthusiastically. If she would like to have that experience herself, he offered to take her up in his Brequet.

Very early the next morning, Victoria and Z. set off in the dark in his small combat plane. With two open cockpits, a deafening motor, and a violent wind, it was a whole new world for her. Fear and then panic turned to rapturous excitement as Victoria experienced the sensation of space. There was no doubt she was impressed by Z.'s daring maneuvers and thoroughly exhilarated by her aerial baptism.

When she told Julian about this escapade, his reaction was far from supportive. He was furious that she would have taken such chances, and without even telling him. From then on Victoria had the uneasy feeling that things were falling apart between them.

Later, after Z. kissed Victoria in a taxi (and, she added, "that was all"), she was filled with remorse and self-reproach. But she didn't tell Julian about it and continued to see Z. Her silence became even more of a threat. A wall, held together by psychological cement, was slowly being built between the two lovers.

They were now completely out of phase and seldom spoke to one another. Meanwhile Victoria began to develop an aversion for Z. She went to Julian, asked his forgiveness, and told him, once again, that she loved only him. At this point Victoria was frantic. Julian's response was a sudden, rare anger.

. . . "I don't want explanations or details. Don't adorn me with your noble interpretations of something that is extremely vulgar. You want to make love to this man. Well, go ahead. Don't feel inhibited. But spare me all this playacting—and stop whimpering! "You lied when you said you loved me, and I believed you. What an imbecile! Now I'm asking you to let me go. I won't come back either tomorrow or the day after tomorrow or anytime this month. And don't try to telephone me because it will be useless. Let go of my arm or I'll hurt you."

I spent some interminable days, the most suffocating I've ever known in love. . . . I went from burning remorse to furious, painful rebellion. When I thought about how I had behaved I felt despicable and I realized the punishment was fair. I wanted to accept it calmly, as an expiation. But I couldn't endure J.'s absence.

When, on the other hand, I began judging him I thought: "I wonder how many women have lain in his arms before he knew me! I've suffered because of each one of those affairs, no matter how insignificant they may have been. I've suffered in silence, in secret. I've spent days driven crazy by retrospective jealousy, jealousy for each one of J.'s women, of women so diverse and numerous that they become as jarring to the heart as the speed of solar light is to our imagination. Three hundred thousand kilometers every second. . . . Three hundred thousand kilometers of unknown, lying women, recreating what for him had been nothing: an orgasm soon forgotten in another orgasm!"

⚮

[In despair] I arrived at Julian's apartment with a revolver in my purse. A revolver I had no idea how to use. But at least I knew how to press the trigger. The idea of having a revolver gave me relief. I was hoping that the gun would symbolize my state of mind, my determination to die if I didn't win him back. I was hoping it would soften J.'s feelings for me. I was wrong. J. declared once again that this was pure extortion and that he despised such a ridiculous means of coercion. He spoke the truth and I knew it. I also knew how inflexible he could be. Not even the threat of my suicide could move him. I would have to find some other way. To wait. To wait for him. But waiting was the one thing I never felt capable of doing. To wait for him to calm down. This time I waited.

I remember it still: we were in his car and he was going to let me off on some deserted street. Overcome, turning aside pleadings and protests, I was silent. Soon, one of his hands left the wheel and his arm went around my shoulder, he pulled me over and pressed me close. He went on driving with one hand without saying a word. I kissed the hand that was near my lips, without daring to speak, or to cry, or even to move. I was coming on tiptoes upon a happiness that, once threatened, I hadn't believed would be retrievable. The gesture of that arm has stayed alive in me through time, separation, and death. (A,3:91–94)

But the reconciliation only lasted a short while; their relationship was already irreparably damaged. Victoria's years with Julian, years that truly transformed her life, were coming to a close.

For Victoria there would be other lovers, but she would always think of Julian as the greatest love of her life. And, also, of the affair as a vital learning experience.

Now as I look back . . . it seems to me that in order to understand the laws of the human condition—and other laws with no name, which however do exist—I had to receive the baptism of this fire, of this kind of love. I received it neither too soon nor too late, at a time when I was able to live fully all that this love revealed to me. (A,3:143–44)

Young and resilient, Victoria slowly emerged from her series of melodramatic crises with Julian. She was resolved to put her life together again, to set out in new directions. The process of self-reflection revealed that her encounter with passionate love had released powerful forces that she was determined to tame, to channel, and to transform into something constructive.

Getting Started as a Writer

DANTE AND EARLY CRITICISM

In this frame of mind, Victoria turned again to Dante's *The Divine Comedy,* which she had first read in Paris with such exhilaration.

> I had just turned sixteen when my Italian professor had me read some passages from "The Inferno." My reaction to that reading can only be compared to the sensation I had as a small child when I went swimming in the ocean for the first time and was tumbled over and over in the sand by the magnificent force of a wave. (FB:32)

Now as she approached thirty, Victoria hoped that Dante, so familiar with sins and suffering, would provide her with insights, perhaps some healing advice. She was looking for a spiritual way, beyond the passionate love she had known, and her autobiography now takes on a reflective tone.

> In religious orders, when a person takes the vow of chastity, it is positively necessary, I think, not to be castrated: to be a whole person for whom chastity doesn't signify impotence. The relevant, estimable thing for me during those years was that my urgent need for spiritual values, that I would glean from the great contemporary religious figures, did not coincide at all with any distaste or weariness of the senses, with the dimming or dulling of sexual appetite that is the fatal consequence of time. That need flourished. My spiritual journey began at the height of my animal life, of a love life that had been fully satisfied and shared. (A,3:99)

As she read Dante again, Victoria began to appreciate his portrayal of profane and sacred love. She did not miss the parallels between her own experience with Julian and that of Francesca and Paolo, caught in a hurricane, spinning round and round in tormented punishment.

> They are wrapped in each other's arms, but blind and deaf to one another. Solitary prisoners of the storm and the night. Prisoners of their own storm and their own night. (FB:34)

Julian had encouraged her to write about her interpretation of *The Divine Comedy* and this act of writing became a catharsis for her shattered psyche. Before long Victoria realized that she did not want to write in a vacuum, but really hoped that her words would reach an audience. As she began to feel the need for outside input, she found two literary critics, both friends of her family, who read her manuscript. The first, Ángel de Estrada, cautioned her that her own scandalous experience would be transparent, and he warned her that the public would be put off by her too direct, too personal style. He counseled her to adopt a veil of literary modesty.

The second reader was Paul Groussac, a well-known and sometimes feared critic of the Argentine literary scene. His letter in reaction to Victoria's manuscript was even more disturbing. He implied that her talent was limited; he belittled her attempt to comment on such a lofty subject, saying that she offered nothing new to scholars. He made it clear that he found her choice of subject, Dante, an exalted figure of the European literary tradition, an uninvited intrusion into the male literary domain—reserved for scholarly writers like himself. He advised her to choose a more personal subject, something less classical, less demanding—something more suitable for a woman.

This first experience with criticism of her work was a decided setback for Victoria's budding ambition. Groussac's words made her "feel withered, like a hydrangea after a day in the north wind" (FB:11). Julian tried to comfort her. He told her that she would be lost if she gave up in the face of the least opposition and he advised her to pay no attention to her critics. Victoria never forgot Groussac's harsh words and they contributed to her lifelong defensiveness about her writing. Even years later she kept responding to Groussac's criticism in her essays. In her sixties Victoria reflected that this criticism, so jolting at the time, was just what she might have expected.

In those years, the attitude of Argentine "society" toward a woman writer wasn't exactly indulgent. What Jane Austen said in the nineteenth century was still true: A woman, if she has the misfortune to know something, should hide it as carefully as she can. It was just as scandalous in my day for a woman to be a writer as to drive her own car through the streets of Buenos Aires. For this last I was showered with a plentiful rain of insults (A,3:105)

EARLY ESSAYS

Victoria was hurt but not deterred. She rallied a stubborn drive, a determination to persist as a writer. On April 4, 1920, three days before her thirtieth birthday, her first essay, "Babel," was published in Buenos Aires' prestigious daily newspaper, *La Nación*. It was written in French and signed, to accommodate public expectations, with her married name, Victoria Ocampo de Estrada.

In this debut as a published writer, Victoria showed how intrepid she could be. Taking as her text the Genesis story of the Tower of Babel, Victoria suggested that the Eternal One had been much too severe in His punishment of Noah's children, perhaps because Jehovah himself was unaware of the dreadful repercussions it would have on future generations. Her audacity does not stop there; "this dirty trick," she called it. For, as she saw it, we still "continue throwing the same words at one another, words whose content differs just as we differ from one another," and we are left with a Babel of voices raised in endless interpretations and contributing little to understanding (E-1:47).

Victoria was unconventional as she considered the word *equality*, "a big word, swollen with emptiness, that we toss around a lot." The concept of Equality, she wrote, obscures an injustice and is not compatible with either Liberty or Fraternity. She then cited Jesus who in the beatitudes said, "Blessed are those who hunger and thirst for justice" (Matthew 5:1–12). But, she pointed out, "He made no mention of equality because the hunger and thirst for equality couldn't be satisfied since human beings are not all the same." Indeed, she added, there is a secret happiness and justice in inequality when we learn to be satisfied with ourselves and our own levels of achievement and accept the fact that some people will be more talented than us in certain areas, some less.

The editors of *La Nación* were delighted with "Babel" and appended a comment praising her talent and expressing their regret that the writer's unjustified reticence had kept her from submitting earlier samples of her work. But Victoria's parents were astonished and dismayed when they read the essay in the morning paper. They felt she had treated the Eternal One with a lack of respect and were shocked by the public display of their daughter's thoughts and feelings. This was not the path they had expected her to follow; they were as apprehensive about her future, she reported, as if she were venturing into a land inhabited by cannibals.[1]

The following month, Victoria wrote an essay about Ruskin for *La Nación* (E-2). At first she lauded the renowned English art critic for having said that the most marvelous spectacle he had ever seen—more impressive even than a perfect work of art—was a human being who also had a brain. But then, in discussing his essay "Sesame," about how to read books and extract their treasures from them, Victoria complained that Ruskin was condescending. She chided him because he did not consider his reader to be an intelligent, thinking being. Why, she wondered, did he deny his reader the right to say, "Ah, that is exactly what I thought"? And she concluded that it was because Ruskin believed that the great truths he proclaimed were reserved for him alone, a superior being. Startling thoughts, daring writing.

These two essays were an auspicious beginning for a woman in those days in Argentina, indeed for anyone, anywhere. But two essays are not enough to assure success. There was no guarantee that she would be taken seriously as an intellectual or as a writer, something for which Victoria knew she yearned. And except for her independence, her defiance, and her tendency to challenge the established patriarchal order, her writing showed, as yet, no certain sign of the latent feminist wielding the pen.

That writer began to emerge in 1921, when Victoria had finished her commentary on Dante, which she called "De Francesca a Beatrice." It too was published in *La Nación,* again in French. She was feeling more confident, she wrote as she pleased and said what she really thought, to the point of challenging her earlier critics, almost to the point of deliberate disregard of their opinions.

In the preface to this commentary Victoria took on Groussac, identifying him as one of "that numerous and terrible band of guards: the commentators" who, she said accusingly, stand "armed with aggressive erudition on the threshold of each canto, . . . brandishing their often contradictory interpretations like pitchforks. . . ." Some of these commentators are "excellent" or "indispensable," she conceded, but there are others who only mislead the reader. Sometimes, she adds, Dante's "dark forest" is dark only because it is so thick with commentators (FB:20).

Victoria then went on to state flatly that she did not believe that great erudition was necessary for the reader to understand and enjoy *The Divine Comedy.* She asserted that Dante was speaking to a wide range of people, not just to an intellectual elite.

Poets, philosophers, theologians, politicians, and lovers, Dante profoundly shakes and moves all these beings, divided by diverse tendencies; he
takes hold of them so preemptively that they each claim him for their own.
No problem, no perplexity, no suffering, no happiness, no aspiration of
the soul or of the human spirit, was alien to Dante. (FB:24)

In the final enthusiastic paragraph of her preface, Victoria defined her aim
in writing the commentary, an aim that, for her, was an act of intellectual rebellion.

I hope to be useful to those who will go through *The Divine Comedy* with
me, in a way—alas!—too fast and superficial. I will try to guide them along
that path which I have journeyed and loved in so many different ways, and
I trust that my tourists will not feel too chagrined when they see how weak
is my means of expression compared to the fervor that spurs me on.
Only a difference in dimension separates the individual drama from
the public drama . . . it is the individual drama, not the public one told in
the pages of *The Divine Comedy,* which concerns me.
I do not address the Danteologists, nor erudite scholars, since I have nothing to teach them. I address the common readers, those who might be able
to love this beautiful, this tremendous book, and who, for one reason or
another, have still not approached it. I address myself, above all, to readers
who have just lazily leafed through it. (FB:25–26)

Victoria had now made it clear that there would be no tiptoeing for her. She
was not afraid to venture into risky territory, to challenge her male critics, to
cite Shakespeare, or to summon up Jesus and the fathers of the church. Indeed,
she was pushing hard on the accepted limits of what a woman, in that time and
place, could hope to articulate in the written word.[2]

Hurdles and Decisions

Victoria chose to have a career as a writer and to create an independent intellectual existence for herself outside the restrictive confines of the life offered
by her conservative family. But it wasn't easy. In Argentina, in the early decades
of the twentieth century, women who aspired to careers faced obstacles that
arose because of the attitudes and practices of the society in which they lived.
Fundamental to an understanding of those times is the realization that women
were then considered to be a step below men; second-class citizens with few

rights and no vote, who needed protection—and surveillance. If a woman chose to be a writer, so much the worse. Society judged women who wrote even more harshly than it did a man of letters.

A man of letters is a phrase that in our society is only used in a pejorative sense. "He is a *literato*" (or worse, "she is a *literata*"), means a cold, useless person, a tramp, even a homosexual (unless he's a professor or holds a university chair; people respect titles like that). If it happens to be a woman, then she is unfailingly blue-stocking, affected, teetering on perversion, and at best an intolerable literary snob, one who appears in a poor light. (A,2:104)

As Victoria began her career as a writer, she had to make the same kinds of decisions all writers make, either consciously or unconsciously. Though she had the ambition, energy, and willpower to bring a proposed project to finished form, she still had to determine her message, her form and style, and her intended audience. Victoria's decisions were unconventional in that they invaded terrain usually reserved for male writers.

She chose to write essays, a traditionally male form. Poetry or letters, a more intimate, more feminine genre, would have been a more acceptable choice. The subjects she chose to write about—literature, music, people, ideas—were similar to the ones chosen by men. It was her style that announced her difference. She sometimes addressed the reader in a familiar way, not in the formal voice that men generally used. She approached topics with an intensely personal, almost conversational style characterized by bounding enthusiasm, a slightly ironic humor, and occasional playfulness. She digressed, she asked questions, she challenged, she drew back and considered her readers' possible opinions.

In keeping with her rejection of the ostentatious display of scholarly trappings, Victoria announced that she wanted to write, not for intellectual critics, but for that person who differs from the critic or erudite reader, who reads exclusively for pleasure, with no anxiety caused by having to reproduce what he has learned—that person whom Samuel Johnson called the common reader.[3] Not too common a reader though; Victoria's Argentine "common reader" would have to be able to read French with ease.

There still remained the troublesome business of finding a publisher. Victoria's first essays were published by *La Nación*, but newspapers are here today and thrown out tomorrow, and Victoria, being ambitious, wanted to put her work between hard covers. It would take a few years for her to find a satisfac-

tory solution to this problem—establishing her own publishing house. Once
she did, a steady stream of her words, stretching over more than forty years, was
assured of finding its way into print.

One of the most perplexing problems that Victoria faced was language.
Though she lived in a Spanish-speaking country, French was really her first language, English her second, and Spanish a weak third. As a child she played,
prayed, and thought in French so it became natural, and more comfortable, for
her to write in that language. But Groussac had been fiercely critical of her writing in French and, of course, there were others too who criticized her for this,
seeing it as a coquettish display of elitism or an arrogant disregard for the
language of Argentina.

Victoria soon realized that if she wanted to build an audience broader than
the limited upper class who read French something would have to change. Her
first solution was to write her essays in French and then have them translated
into Spanish. But the translations irritated her because she didn't recognize herself in them. Her eventual, but painful, answer to the dilemma was to teach herself to translate her essays into an attractive Spanish. This was a process that she
wasn't able to handle confidently until she was in her forties.

Heroes, Mentors, and Friends

In her adolescent years, it was the characters Victoria met in books who became
her first heroes and heroines: courageous adventurers out of Jules Verne, force-
ful characters straight from Dickens, or appealing heroines like Mme. de Staël's
Corinne. Always the actress, Victoria would project herself into a play or novel,
falling in love with some characters and identifying with others. She read avidly
from the works of Conan Doyle, Poe, Racine, Hugo, de Staël, de Maupassant, and Shakespeare, so there was no shortage of material for her latent, if frustrated, acting talent.

Although her early heroes were fictional, around 1924 she began to have
them in the flesh. Most of them were men and only one was an Argentine. They
were writers or philosophers or musicians, and they became temporary or
lifelong heroes for a number of rather complex reasons. First of all, she found
them interesting. They expanded her horizons and she was pleased when they
took her seriously as an intelligent woman. Like an actress taking curtain calls,
she enjoyed being in the spotlight of their fame. But there is more to it than
that. Victoria needed these associations with famous people to bolster her
self-confidence; to counter an underlying feeling of inferiority that might be

traced back to her experiences with Franky and the other boys she played with as a young girl, to the cutting criticism of Estrada and Groussac, and perhaps also to her gnawing sense that Argentina's culture was inferior to that of Europe. Victoria used her position as a wealthy and beautiful young woman to create opportunities to meet men from whom, whatever their initial interest in her, she could draw intellectual stimulus.

ORTEGA

In 1916 Victoria met José Ortega y Gasset while he was on a lecture tour in Argentina. From the start, she was in awe of him, impressed by his erudition, his sensitivity to ideas, and perhaps, too, by the fame he had already won as a writer. He was attracted by the Victoria he saw, for she was quite a beauty.

> I had a subtle, special beauty, the kind that a shared love gives a woman: the kind that comes from a man and that she feels because of him. Her being radiates happiness. That was the cosmetic that made me beautiful. It was on my skin, in my eyes, in my smile, it circulated through my blood. (A,3:108–9)

Later, in a letter to Victoria, Ortega was to recall meeting her for the first time. She was wearing a broad-brimmed straw hat and "her eyes reflect the energetic fever of a prisoner and she is withdrawn, timid, showing a lack of interest in the man who has just arrived. She gave me the impression of a little girl." A while later he amended this description with his discovery that "beneath the withdrawn little girl appeared a very strong, passionate femininity" (A,3:114).

Victoria was elated that Ortega seemed to regard her as a thinking woman, but it is clear that her beauty played no small part in this ripening friendship. Over the next few days they spent a good deal of time together, Ortega dazzled by her appearance and Victoria overwhelmed by his intellectual magnetism.

> What did we talk about in our early conversations? I don't remember. I listened. What I do recall is that everything he said was said in a special, penetrating way. I remember his way of saying things more than what he said. Ortega took a theme and pursued it, the way a spotlight follows a solo ballerina—with this difference: he was both the spotlight and the ballerina. I contemplated the spectacle and appreciated his mastery. Until then fate had not treated me with a banquet of such magnitude. . . . But perhaps Ortega,

like most men, was not aware of the extent to which I was capable of becoming impassioned (in a different sense than amorous passion) by a book, an idea, a man who personified that book or that idea—without letting my passion invade other zones of my being. (A,3:109–10)

A few days after their first meeting, Ortega's and Victoria's eyes met at a luncheon and he said he encountered the Giaconda of the Pampa. He found this experience "surprising, sudden and explosive." The following day, Ortega was further astonished by an invitation to have dinner at Victoria's house. Until then he had not detected any interest in him on her part. From then on Ortega was enraptured. He portrayed a magnificent Victoria in a black velvet, off-the-shoulder gown, "appearing with all the grace and dignity of a spiritual monument." Victoria became a myth for him—but a real myth, he admits, that began to gravitate to his "transitory heart" (A,3:115–16). He recalls an incredible moment with her as the evening ended and he was standing by the door, ready to leave. At that moment he said to himself:

There can be no doubt. This Gioconda has understood me forever and right down to the toes. She will never confuse me with anyone else. How strange! She *knows* me completely, by heart. She likes the way I completely deform the trivial things life throws at our feet so I can restore them with a new, dancing, rhythmical life. She has discovered that for me life is a matter of style. (A,3:117)

Ortega also detected another, more serious side of Victoria. Referring to her in one of his lectures, he remarked that he did not expect anything from the person who was satisfied with his life and added that his hope had been ignited by an Argentine woman. "I have seen her soul take flight . . . in a sublime, divine, discontent."[4]

After Ortega returned to Spain, Victoria was incensed and wounded when she heard that he had offered the opinion that she was lowering herself by wasting her time with a man of inferior intellect like Julian. Victoria stopped corresponding with Ortega for several years, but at a price. It was anguishing for her to lose the only serious support she had in the literary world.

During the next few years, Victoria would gather strength, confidence, and experience. They were eventful years for her, years that bore the influence of people she knew, books she read and ideas she played with in her mind. She had already begun to show the direction she would go as a writer; now was the time to mature as a woman.

GÜIRALDES

Another man who was important to Victoria was the Argentine writer, Ricardo Güiraldes. Their friendship began in 1915 and by the 1920s had developed into an easy-going Platonic relationship based on their shared background. Their wealthy parents had seen to it that they were fluent in French and at home in Paris. Both were great readers and loved to discuss books, art, music, and poetry. Beyond these similarities they each had a feeling of estrangement from their own culture, which they saw as being materialistic and anti-intellectual. Although they loved Argentina, neither of them felt they fit into the conventional mold of their times.

Güiraldes had written books of poetry, stories, and novels and knew all too well the frustration of having his work severely criticized or totally ignored. Like Victoria, he had felt the stinging rebuke of critics who thought he wrote too much under the influence of French writers and classified him as a "foreignizer."

In the years when Victoria and Julian were living together and seldom ventured out into "society," Ricardo Güiraldes and his wife, Adelina del Carril, were among the friends they used to see and with whom, on Thursday nights, they used to dance the tango. Later, in the twenties, Ricardo and Adelina often came to Victoria's house and read to her from his manuscripts in progress. When his published works failed to excite the critics or the public, Victoria suffered with him. He, in turn, was a comfort to her.

> During those years, Ricardo was the only person to whom I could confide my tribulations. This was because of the pureness of his heart, his capacity for friendship, and his quick understanding, almost without words, of someone else's conflicts. (T,10:108)

In 1924, Güiraldes and a few other writers, among them Jorge Luis Borges, founded a literary magazine, *Proa,* with the hope of bringing new life to Argentine literature. Victoria watched as Güiraldes devoted his time and energy to *Proa,* only to have it fail a year later. But his commitment to the journal and his perseverance, despite the unwelcoming intellectual environment of Buenos Aires, were not lost on Victoria and she would remember his example a few years later as she faced the challenge of founding her own literary journal.

Victoria believed in Güiraldes and rejoiced when, in 1926, his talent was finally recognized. His *Don Segundo Sombra* was published and overnight he awoke to enthusiastic acclaim.[5] With its hints of French impressionistic writing and its embrace of startling metaphors, the novel seemed to Victoria a vindication of the love for French literature that she shared with Güiraldes. It was, at the same time, a convincing display of his strong roots in Argentina. Remembering Güiraldes years later, Victoria wrote:

> He is not for me just the Argentine writer who has given our literature a magnificent story of the gaucho, a classic like the *Martín Fierro* of José Hernández. He is that and much more: he is the friend who, with me, found consolation in the low moments of our lives by reading aloud from the great French poets. He was the most sensitive, responsive, understanding, and noble of the Argentine men whom I have had the good fortune to call brother. (T,10:108)

1924

The year 1924 represented a turning point for Victoria. She sold the house where she had lived out her disastrous marriage, she got rid of a great many of her possessions, and she moved into an apartment. Julian was now only a background presence in her life. Alone and stripped of superfluous material possessions, she experienced a new sense of freedom. She drove her own car (occasionally in scandalous sleeveless dresses), she wore her hair in a bob, and sometimes she even smoked cigarettes.[6] In short, Victoria put herself on display as an independent, rebellious woman who had a mind of her own, a woman who had the confidence to shrug off criticism and go her own nonconforming way.

She continued to struggle with regret and conflict, but life for her was now more stable. She regretted not having had a child with Julian and she regretted never having pursued a career in the theater. But she reconciled herself by saying that her life had been guided by love (for J., for her family) and not by ambition. Now, in 1924, she regretted that her ambitious drive had arisen "so late." Always an undercurrent in her life, ambition was finally coming into play, and although she did not fully know how her ambition would be directed, she sensed that a new phase of her life was beginning.

In 1924, through Ortega's publishing house in Madrid, Victoria saw her commentary on Dante come alive in print. For in 1921, years after Ortega and Victoria had stopped corresponding, a friend had sent a copy of Victoria's essay "Babel" to him in Spain. Ortega was impressed by her talent and her extraordinary style and asked to see anything else she had written. In response, Ortega was sent her essay on Dante. Ortega was enthusiastic about it, had it translated from French to Spanish, and then had it published by his own Madrid press, Revista de Occidente. Her book became a small volume of less than one hundred pages bearing the title *De Francesca a Beatrice.* It was dedicated to Julian.

The publication was a lucky break for Victoria. She was grateful to Ortega and gave him credit for being so generous to her in the face of her own stubborn silence. And so, after long years of interruption, their friendship and their correspondence resumed. It lasted until Ortega's death in 1955 and was of major significance in helping to shape Victoria's career.

While 1924 was notable because of the publication of the Dante commentary, it was also important because three men of strong influence entered her life: Mohandas Gandhi, Rabindranath Tagore, and Ernest Ansermet. With them, she said, contemporary India and modern music burst upon her life.

GANDHI

Early in 1924 Victoria had the pivotal experience of reading Romain Rolland's biography of Gandhi. She was tremendously impressed by Gandhi's spiritual message, by his rebellion against the misery he saw around him, by his decision to resort to noncooperation as his defense against the British, and by his willingness to be imprisoned for his convictions. She was "inspired with respect and exaltation" by this ascetic leader, this rare example of "a great man who lived as he believed. (A,4:17). In March of that year, after she read an article in a British newspaper calling Gandhi a fanatical agitator, she wrote an essay for *La Nación* introducing the Gandhi she knew from his biography. In later years she would write more articles about Gandhi; she was now devoted to him and his commitment to nonviolent resistance. He would become one of the most important influences on her thinking.

TAGORE

Among intellectuals in Buenos Aires in 1924, the Indian poet Rabindranath Tagore was all the rage, almost a cult figure. When his collection of poems *Gitanjali,* for which he had won the Nobel Prize for Literature in 1913, was translated into Spanish, readers in Argentina were intrigued by what for many of them was their first contact with India.

Victoria had read *Gitanjali* in 1914, in André Gide's "wonderful" French translation, and said that his poetry "fell like celestial dew on my anguishing twenty-four-year-old heart." (A,4:18). As she reread Tagore's poetry ten years later, she was once again enthralled by what she called his magical mysticism.

She felt powerful echoes in Tagore's personal, loving God who radiated happiness and serenity, so unlike the vengeful, demanding God imposed on her in childhood.

From the moment it was announced that Tagore would stop in Buenos Aires on his way to Peru, Victoria anticipated his arrival with tremendous excitement. The newspapers proclaimed that his visit would be the great event of the year in Buenos Aires; Victoria said later that for her it was one of the great events of her life.

Even before she knew Tagore, Victoria showed that she had begun to grasp the wisdom of his religious works. She felt strongly that Western readers of Tagore needed no special preparation except spiritual maturity to understand his words about love.

> The spring of 1924 in San Isidro was clear and warm with roses. I spent the mornings in my room with the windows open, reading Tagore, thinking about Tagore, writing Tagore letters I would never send. From this reading, thinking, waiting, and writing were born those pages of mine that *La Nación* published. (TB:15)[7]

Victoria began this essay, written just before Tagore arrived, distinguishing the joy one feels on reading Tagore from the pleasure experienced after reading Proust's *Remembrance of Things Past*.

> To enter into the world of Tagore's poems after emerging from Proust's novel is like a bath to the weary, dust-covered traveler after crossing the desert. It is to breathe pure air beneath a grand old tree after a prolonged stay in a great city. A beautiful, fascinating city, but one that exudes pollution. It is to sit down in a friend's house after an exhausting day spent with strangers who are so attentive to our fragmentary truths that they miss the total sum of our being. (TB:20)

When Tagore's ship landed in Buenos Aires, he was too tired and too sick with flu to continue on to Peru. He had just returned from lecturing in China and Japan and was exhausted. He needed, the doctors said, rest and a chance to regain his strength. When Victoria heard this, she invited Tagore to stay as her guest at a house in San Isidro, where he could have the peace and quiet he needed.

Tagore soon settled into a happy routine on the banks of the River Plata, writing poetry, reading, watching the birds and the changing color of the river, dining with Victoria, and often strolling with her in the garden. Frequently Victoria was among the many visitors who sat at the master's feet under the ombu tree, listening to him talk. She found great pleasure in putting fresh flowers in his room, in making sure his clothes were in good order and that he was eating healthy food. She accompanied him when he wanted company and stayed away when she sensed he preferred to be alone. She translated for him if his visitors didn't understand English and sent them away if she thought he was getting tired. In a hundred small ways, she mothered, she monitored, she attended Tagore and soon developed for him a tender, admiring friendship that was reciprocated from the beginning.

Victoria was overawed by Tagore and mostly just listened to him. Tagore too had problems expressing himself, perhaps because he didn't realize that a young woman, "dressed in white, in yellow, in pink, who sat at his side every day," might be concerned with serious ideas (A,4:34). There was a grandeur, a gentleness about him—and a twinkle in his eye—that Victoria found attractive. She called him Gurudev (Master) and was happy to sit at his feet and to serve him.

But, of course, they did talk together and they found they had things in common: their personal, passionate approaches to Shakespeare and religion and nature, their discomfort with authority and mistrust of tyrants. Their conversations were an important intellectual stimulus for Victoria and gradually their relationship developed into a bond of mutual affection. For there is no mistaking the affection that is reflected in their letters to each other and in the love poems he wrote for her. Indeed, Tagore's book of love poems, *Puravi,* is dedicated to Victoria.

The impact on Victoria of Tagore's visit to Argentina was profound and beneficial. By 1924 Victoria was able to turn her focus outward onto the world beyond Argentina. Tagore, like Gandhi, alerted Victoria to international problems and to India's struggle for independence. Reading all of Tagore's books, she became familiar with the Upanishads, with eternal, universal truths, and with the idea of the greatness and invincibility of the human spirit. She found in Tagore's words similarities with the teachings of the Gospels and St. Thomas Aquinas, and was both impressed and moved.

Tagore also gave Victoria reason to reconsider the relationship between men and women. She found in his novels, plays, and poetry no entertainment of the concept of equality between the sexes. In his works, Tagore seemed to subscribe to the idea that woman's creative destiny would be fulfilled by becoming the energizing inspiration for the endeavors of men. Indeed, Victoria became the muse of Tagore's remaining years, inspiring a great deal of his poetic creativity.

Tagore, though lovable, was not the guide Victoria needed, for his outlook was not one she could accept. She would have to have further experiences before she could arrive at the underlying philosophy that informs her essays on women.

Tagore's presence also made Victoria aware of the ways in which foreigners perceived Argentina. He alerted her to questions of Argentina's national identity and brought home to her the difficulty of translating a culture for foreign eyes. His words prodded Victoria to begin thinking of Argentina as a part of a much larger world and stimulated her to consider ways to bridge the cultural distances that separate nations.

Perhaps the most subtle influence Tagore had on Victoria was that he gave her some understanding of what it was to have a sense of mission, for he had applied a feeling of duty to himself when he left Argentina to return to his work in India. He later wrote Victoria that he hoped she would find some work in her life that would be worthy of his love for her. Altogether, at this rather turbulent time in her life, Tagore seems to have had a calming effect on Victoria and to have given her a new serenity and self-confidence.

As Tagore sailed away on January 4, 1925, Victoria was overcome with sadness. They wrote back and forth all through 1925, letters expressing their nostalgia for the days that Tagore described as his "easeful captivity" in San Isidro. But the frequency of their correspondence diminished as time went on and there is an unexplained hiatus in communication between 1926 and 1929. Several times Tagore wrote to Victoria asking her to meet him in Europe, pleading with her to come to India, but she never seemed able to fit such a trip into her schedule. It was only by coincidence that they met again, in France, and for the last time, in 1930. It is not surprising that Victoria's relationship with Tagore gradually died down and almost faded away since the next few years of her life became rather suddenly full of interesting new experiences and people. There would have been little time, or intensity, left over for Tagore.

ANSERMET

Victoria's success in playing secretary-hostess to Tagore led her to think that she had discovered her true vocation. She felt encouraged that she might do the same for other great writers or cultural giants and use this as a vehicle for her own intellectual growth. At this time Victoria envisioned herself as a patron of the arts in general and creative people in particular. She regretted that there were not enough wealthy people in Buenos Aires who were willing to underwrite a vigorous cultural life there. But she had both enough money and the right connections to make a difference and she decided to use them for this purpose.

In 1924 the Swiss conductor Ernest Ansermet, fresh from conducting the Ballets Russes in Europe, came to Buenos Aires to conduct the maiden performances of a newly formed orchestra. Victoria was impressed by him when she heard one of his concerts; she invited him to lunch. Before long they became involved in the exciting possibilities of establishing in Buenos Aires a first-rate symphony orchestra that he might conduct. When Victoria tried to persuade Ansermet to return to Argentina for another season, she took up the cause of her country and the development of its cultural life and argued that

> his work with us in Argentina, although obscure and poorly remunerated, was infinitely more important that what he might do in Paris, Berlin, Brussels, etc. Here he was shaping the taste of a new public, he was forming an orchestra, training musicians. . . . For our country it was the epoch for sowing seed. (A,4:95–96)

When Ansermet returned the following season, he and Victoria met almost daily at her house for lunch or dinner. From the start the musician regarded Victoria seriously as an intellectual. He read her essay on Tagore, read Proust aloud to her, played the piano for her, listened to records with her, and for hours at a time discussed modern music, poetry, religion, Shakespeare—as well as people he knew: Stravinsky, Debussy, Diaghilev, Nijinsky, and Cocteau.

As usual, Victoria rode her enthusiasm to its fullest. She became a generous and faithful supporter of the orchestra, prevailing on her friend Marcelo Alvear, then president of Argentina, to give the orchestra sufficient support to ensure its survival. She never missed an orchestra rehearsal and was excited by the kinds of avant-garde music that Ansermet was introducing to Buenos Aires. When he asked her to be the narrator for a production of Honegger's "King David," she was thrilled. It was the first time that a woman had taken this part and for Victoria the performance, in French, was a truly triumphant experience.

> I believe that nothing in the world has given me such happiness, from the point of view of artistic realization, as I felt when I interpreted "King David" with Ansermet. I expressed myself fully, entirely. And I *communicated.* . . . I had the sensation of holding the audience in the palm of my hand. . . . The intoxication I experienced has no parallel. It seemed to me that the com-

munication that was established between the audience and me enriched me with the vitality and energy of each person there. I was multiplied by hundreds of beings who were converting themselves into me. (A,4:103–4)

By 1927 the orchestra seemed to be established, even though much of its audience was not comfortable with the unfamiliar, modern music that Ansermet chose to play. Victoria had helped to raise money for the orchestra and optimistically thought that it was now on firm enough footing to pay Ansermet the salary he deserved. Instead, she records, "Catastrophe." The orchestra board refused to reappoint Ansermet, and instead engaged a man named Hadley, a little-known North American conductor. Victoria, who was on the board, was stunned, but she quickly discovered that the mostly male members of the board felt no desire to have a female meddling in their business. Some of this feeling turned personally on Victoria, with criticism directed at her unconventional lifestyle. When Victoria saw that she wasn't able to change their stand, she wrote them a violent letter and resigned from the board with a resounding slamming of the door. She was, she said, terribly disillusioned and angry and she spoke ambivalently of Argentina as her ungrateful and beloved country. She even threatened to leave and move to Europe.

This might have been the end of Victoria's constructive life in Argentina had it not been for Ansermet. He wrote to persuade her that the vision and efforts of one individual really do count. He urged her to continue to support Argentina's cultural life. And most importantly he emphasized that she must establish her mark, in her own way, in her own country.

MAEZTU

The intellectuals of Buenos Aires society had long been fond of inviting famous people from abroad to come to Argentina on lecture tours, for there was a deep and continuing thirst for culture in this relatively isolated country. Le Corbusier, Ortega, and Tagore are notable examples of lecturers who came to Argentina in the 1920s. There would be many others, including Herman Keyserling and Waldo Frank; among them would be an important woman, María de Maeztu.

In 1926 Victoria herself had begun to give occasional lectures before intimate cultural groups like the Amigos de Arte. After one of her early lectures, a small woman came up to Victoria, shook her hand effusively, and introduced herself as María de Maeztu. Maeztu was an educator from Spain and an outright feminist who had come to Buenos Aires to give a series of lectures sponsored by the Spanish Cultural Institute. She had received an outstanding education in literature and philosophy, had a doctorate from the University of Salamanca, had studied with Ortega, and had done research at Oxford and in Paris. In 1915, in an attempt to improve women's opportunities for higher education in Spain, she put her training in pedagogy to work and founded the College for Women in Madrid. Three years later she started a coeducational primary school. These were both innovative changes in the Spanish educational system. Later she taught at Spanish, Argentine, and North American colleges and universities, including Bryn Mawr, Johns Hopkins, Smith, and Wellesley.

Here was an articulate and informed woman, full of energy and ideas, who believed that women were not just passive objects, but creative, intelligent beings. Victoria and Maeztu soon became friends.

> Not only at the lectures she gave during her first visit to us, but in my house, where she soon grew accustomed to coming daily, María de Maeztu talked and I listened. I led her to those subjects that interested me (the education of women, for example) and I listened untiringly. . . . Our favorite subject—to which we continually returned—was the emancipation of women. To me emancipation was synonymous with education and María had a great deal to teach me in that respect. (E-10:270)

Victoria and Maeztu started from the fact that public opinion seemed only concerned with the problems of men—since men controlled the agenda. They then went on to the inequality of the sexes before the law and in education. They talked about Emmanuel Mounier's concept of the spiritual proletariat of women, those oppressed women (rich and poor, workers and peasants) who found it impossible to shape their own lives. They agreed that the emancipation of women would come during this century, and then they talked about what would happen in the days after emancipation.

> If education and training do not accompany emancipation, liberation will serve no purpose. Ignorance will cancel out or distort its effects. It is, then, fundamental and urgent, terribly urgent, that women receive an education, a training, that is just as carefully planned as that of men. (E-10:271)

Victoria admired Maeztu for being so organized and persevering, for being a steady flow of activity and for struggling to advance an idea in which she fervently believed. Victoria eagerly absorbed her ideas, but because she still did not feel sufficiently articulate or confident of herself to speak out on these matters, Victoria exhorted Maeztu to be a spokesman for the cause of women: "Speak out about it, you who know how to speak. Tell about it on the right and on the left, to the north and to the south. For God's sake, express your opinions" (E-10:272). It would take time and more experience before Victoria herself would speak out on these matters. And even then she would often do so by invoking the authority of some other woman, most notably Virginia Woolf.

KEYSERLING

Although Victoria believed she was unsophisticated when it came to philosophy, in 1927 she began to read the work of Herman Keyserling, which she had come across in a copy of Ortega's literary journal *Revista de Occidente*.[8] Keyserling, a German philosopher, had recently won fame as a world traveler, lecturer, and writer. Victoria's autobiography records her increasing enthusiasm for Keyserling's work. It introduced her to new ideas and made her constantly reexamine her beliefs. She felt a kind of euphoria and a growing confidence as she realized that this man whom she so admired was expressing ideas that she had played with but had never articulated. Clearly, Victoria perceived Keyserling as a mentor who would encourage her intellectual and spiritual growth.

Her enthusiasm soon escalated theatrically into idolatrous fervor. Always a great letter writer, she now began a correspondence with Keyserling, inviting him to come to Buenos Aires to lecture, and, characteristically, offering to have him stay at her house. Keyserling answered that he was all booked up until 1929. Victoria wired back: "Impossible to foresee if enthusiasm will last until then" (EV:24).

Keyserling did agree to come in 1929, and soon their correspondence was in full bloom. Victoria says she wrote about everything that interested her at the moment, especially his books.

> My epistolary self took off like a wild pony. . . . Imagine being able to carry on a dialogue, daily, with such an intelligent, famous man—and to receive long answers! . . . I was the child in front of the Christmas tree and he was the tree full of lights that I contemplated, open-mouthed. (EV:31,34)

By the end of 1927 Victoria was writing Keyserling letters of such bubbling adoration that they sound like a teenager's fan letters. Her letter of November 10, 1927, conveys the inflamed, provocative quality of this correspondence.

It is clear that if I hadn't lived and suffered through certain things (or to be more exact, the lack of certain things) with an atrocious awareness, I would not, at this moment, experience the happiness that I feel on receiving your three letters. . . .

Oh the sunshine of your letters! Let me sleep on them, let me linger over them. And then I will flourish because of them. Ah! How good, how sweet it is. How I love them! I don't know how to talk to you sensibly tonight. I have a headache, but I at least want to write you because tomorrow the transatlantic mail ship sails.[9] And besides, I am so close to you at this moment. . . .

I seem to be so full of what you are that my least movement would make me give off some of your precious aroma. If you were here with me, I would not raise my eyes to your eyes, for fear of losing that "you" who is beneath my jealously closed eyelids.

"I am there," you write me. . . . Isn't it beautiful, isn't it miraculous that those three words resting on my heart comfort me? (A,4:140)

Before long Keyserling was sending Victoria proofs of his latest book. She responded with the suggestion that it be translated into Spanish. Telegrams crossed the Atlantic. Victoria interceded with Spanish publishers, and she even contacted Ortega in hopes that he would facilitate the translation of Keyserling's new book. Contracts followed and Victoria was prepared to make a sizable advance to have the work published. Without perhaps realizing it, Victoria was beginning to be a literary entrepreneur.

Keyserling quite obviously thought of Victoria as a rich young woman, available as a patron, and, apparently too, available as a woman—a rare opportunity that he hoped to exploit. Soon he was urging Victoria to come to Paris so they could discuss his tour of Argentina, so she could teach him Spanish, so they could get to know one another better. Victoria ignored warnings from Maeztu and Ortega about Keyserling's difficult personality and agreed to meet him in Versailles. She wrote him that she would take care of all his expenses.

Keyserling responded with a set of conditions for the visit that he expected Victoria to follow closely. Above all, he stipulated that during his month in France she was to visit him as often as possible. She was not to have a distracting social life on the side; she was to invite him to dinner in Paris once or twice with a select group of Argentines and on those occasions the women were to wear evening clothes, the men tuxedos. Oysters and champagne should be served. Victoria recorded that these requests seemed innocent enough, though she confessed that she detested oysters, champagne, and dinners where you have to dress.

Finally, in December of 1928, amid copious tears as she parted from her family, Victoria sailed off to meet Keyserling in Versailles. She later wrote that she had that uneasy feeling you sometimes have the night before an exam. But, anxious or not, she was on her way. And who could blame Keyserling if he awaited her with great expectations?

Free and alone in Paris, Victoria was overcome with happiness. She went back to the places she loved, the Place de la Concorde, the Champs-Elysées, the Seine, the Arc de Triomphe, the Eiffel Tower. She had tea at Rumpel's and went to a concert that Ansermet conducted. And then she went to Coco Chanel's establishment and ordered a couple of new outfits for her encounter in Versailles.

> Chanel had had an affair with J. in 1913 and I had been jealous of her, as I was of many other women. But now that feeling has been softened by my own happiness. (A,4:150)[10]

Next, Victoria went to Versailles to reserve a suite of rooms for Keyserling at the Hôtel des Réservoir. There she put soap, eau de cologne, and flowers, as well as the large envelopes, blotter, and red ink that he had asked her to buy. At midnight on January 3 she wrote him a letter that would be waiting for him when he arrived at the hotel on January 5.

> I've just come back from seeing Diaghilev's ballets. I loved them so in 1913. I like them even more now. . . . For five minutes at the ballet I forgot all about you.
>
> . . . It seems to me that I am almost saying good-bye on this piece of paper. "Adiós" to that man who you were for me, and who will stop being "that man" in a few hours, in Versailles. How will I manage without that Keyserling of mine, invented by me? (A,4:157–58)

Victoria claimed that 1929 was another turning point in her life. It began the day she actually met Keyserling and the relationship she had imagined was replaced by a real one. Victoria recalled it vividly, perceiving herself in various stages of expectation.

> On January 5, 1929, around four in the afternoon, I looked myself over in the mirror. . . . I was wearing a new sweater, blue, rose and maroon (Chanel), and a tailored navy blue suit, very simple, but very expensive and harder

to find than a ball gown. A felt hat, pulled down to the eyebrows, encircled my head. Lucienne (Reboux) had just cut my hair . . . it was short. The hat was becoming. The tones of the pullover brought out the bronze tone that eighteen days of crossing the Atlantic had given me. (A,5:9)

That woman who was looking at herself in the mirror . . . that day in 1929 was a woman who had come to the end of one stage of her life. . . . I was leaving a safe harbor that had sheltered me for many years; that had strengthened me but also made me languish. . . . two voices were dictating different orders to me: one that I should take refuge at whatever cost in the security of an uncomplicated happiness. . . . The other voice shouted: "Lord preserve us from the numbing effect of sheltered harbors. Force us, Lord, to let go. . . ." . . . this passion of mine had revealed itself to be a trampoline. It was vibrating, elastic, like the tip of a diving board suspended over the emptiness under the feet of the diver who was about to plunge into the water. I was on a trampoline and, having run a race and lost my breath, I was being catapulted toward the void by my own propulsion and condemned to the perilous fall. . . . To where? At what risk? (A,5:19–21)

As Victoria beheld Keyserling for the first time, she saw him as a giant, as Pantagruel: as a threatening presence.

From the first handshake, from the first greeting—a cordial embrace (for the moment)—I had a premonition that I had gotten myself into an awful mess. . . . I found myself squarely in front of a man-eater looking for a more substantial meal. . . . I decided not to let myself be devoured by him, but neither did I want to hurt him or irritate him (idiot that I was). (A,5:9–10,23)

She sensed the sexually predatory nature of his interest and imagined that he saw her as the women he had described in *The Travel Diary of a Philosopher*—a woman who is neither housewife nor prostitute, but a muse, the kind of woman that men need to inspire them to high levels of cultural refinement, women like those who reached an exceptional level during the great periods of Roman civilization. "Yes," she thought to herself, "it is thanks to these women that on the coarse canvas of sexual appetites, man has woven exquisite, silky tapestries" (A,5:11).

Victoria rapidly became disillusioned by this man she had invented and idolized. True, he was an engaging conversationalist, but over the next four weeks, as she visited him almost daily, she saw that he was a glutton and a heavy drinker and that he was outrageously imperious, given to bursts of violent temper, and intolerant of her if she disagreed with him—or worse, if she rejected his advances. Why, she asked herself naively, had this man gotten it into his head to fall in love with her?

Victoria later confessed that if she had loved him she would gladly have submitted to him. But, instead, he revolted her, and she regarded the idea of sex with him as inconceivable. She adopted a strategy of passive resistance in response to his eager advances. She didn't explode in horror, she said, but followed a milder course because she lacked the courage to be frank and cut him off completely. In any case, he was her guest and she felt she should put up with him. A possible additional interpretation that she did not articulate is that she was still determined to bring him to Buenos Aires for the series of lectures she had arranged and that she imagined might bring some glory to herself, as well as to Argentina. And so, once again, and not for the last time, her ambitions would shade her actions.

> Little by little I rejected his program: a perfect union, crowned (O Holy God!) by the union of the flesh. But I believe that, way down deep, this was nothing more for Keyserling than an affair deferred. He must have thought that things would work out in Buenos Aires. (A,5:31)

As Victoria's intense relationship with Keyserling was cooling down, she began to see that he and she were two very different people: one a gifted speaker, avid to talk; the other, almost mute, eager to listen. As with Tagore, Victoria suffered from feeling inarticulate with someone of Keyserling's imagined greatness.

> When I want to express myself, I am slow; I feel suddenly bereft of means, deprived of experience, as if generations and generations of beings who only practiced silence were weighing me down. (EV:44)

Despite her disillusionment, Victoria had to admit that knowing Keyserling had been an exhilarating and expanding experience. Indeed, it had a number of positive outcomes. She found great pleasure in reading his works and being exposed to his ideas. Meeting him had helped her further define herself as a woman. It had forced her to break free of family ties and put further distance between herself and Julian, with whom she was now "just friends." And after she left Versailles she took advantage of being in Europe and traveled a great deal, meeting many new people, several of whom would have a strong influence on her later career. Victoria's experience with Keyserling also put into focus the dangerous aspect of her cult of authors. She was forced to realize that her inveterate need for hero worship was capable of getting her into deep trouble. By now she was thoroughly disgusted with the role of secretary-hostess.

Perhaps the most significant result of Victoria's experience with Keyserling was that she had to confront a different perception of the relationship between men and women and to consider more seriously her own views on women. Not surprisingly, Victoria rejected Keyserling's too rigidly dichotomous conception of man as the active doer, a civilized being who represents intellectual values, and of woman, his complete opposite, a passive creature, primordial in nature, who, in her highest form, nurtured the spiritual side of man's life. She also adamantly opposed his notion that man is superior to woman because he is the bearer of the sperm. She denounced what she saw as his contempt for ordinary women, whom he usually spoke of only as they might meet men's need to reproduce or to find pleasure. Victoria took exception to Keyserling's belief that a man needed three kinds of women: the mother of guaranteed pedigree, the prostitute or courtesan, and, in between, for the inspired, sublime moments in his life, the muse. First Ortega, then Tagore, and now Keyserling—Victoria had had about enough of seeing herself cast in the role of muse.

She recognized that she had learned from this experience, and acknowledging that her early letters to Keyserling went overboard in their enthusiasm, she eventually assumed the blame for the whole fiasco, though she continued to feel that she had been misunderstood by Keyserling. When she later asked herself if she would ever learn to be prudent, she answered, honestly if wistfully, "probably not."

This was not the last chapter in the story of Keyserling and Victoria. A few months later he did come to Argentina for a lecture tour. There were dinners and receptions and he was thoroughly lionized. At Victoria's reception for him at Villa Ocampo, he seemed eloquent and he may have charmed her guests, but Victoria was shocked and furious when she realized that he was half-drunk.

Surrounded by professors, writers, and beautiful women, Keyserling stood there, his hand either on the shoulder or head of Alfonso Reyes, a writer who at the time was the Mexican ambassador to Argentina. (Alfonso seemed minuscule next to Keyserling.) Using Reyes as a cane, Keyserling talked with the hand that held a glass of champagne. As his gestures became more elaborate, the champagne began to spill. His audience,

not to get sprayed, stepped back, the way people on the beach draw back
as a wave approaches. Later, as the orator calmed down, people came closer
once again. (A,6:20)

Victoria was fully chagrined; she left the party and hid in the library.[11]
She thought of Keyserling now as Bacchus and was filled with a hatred as intense as her earlier admiration for him. She returned all his letters, and when
her letters to him were also returned she burned all but a few. A regular auto-
da-fé, she proclaimed. And so in this way the Keyserling phase of Victoria's life
finally seemed to come to an appropriately flaming end.

(But it was not, in fact, the end. Ten years later, in 1939, Keyserling's sister
came to see Victoria in Paris. She told her that her brother was having a very
difficult time in Hitler's Germany. His passport had been taken away, his books
were on a proscribed list, he was prohibited from lecturing; he was a virtual prisoner in his own house. Describing him as a victim of the Third Reich, Keyserling's sister urged Victoria to visit him. Victoria felt she couldn't refuse
and drove to Darmstadt, where she saw Keyserling and had lunch with him the
next day. There in his house, with only a maid who could not speak English,
they were all alone and chose to skirt the past. Keyserling's wife, a Bismarck,
had gone to Hamburg to have lunch with Hitler and try to persuade him to return Keyserling's passport. Victoria observed that Keyserling had lost neither
his appetite nor his thirst for wine.)

A LOVER AND THREE WOMEN

After Keyserling returned to Germany from Versailles, Victoria became thoroughly depressed. She was alone in Paris and unsure of what lay ahead. So
she tried to preserve her friendship with Keyserling by writing him friendly letters. He answered from Germany and even sent her some letters of introduction to writers in Paris and England. Victoria protested that Keyserling's letters
of introduction seemed overblown. "I wanted to present myself to people as I
was, a self-educated, obscure South American woman, a lover of belles lettres
and of Europe, and young enough to be pleasing to the eyes. (A,5:61). But
Victoria was worldly enough to be grateful to Keyserling and to use his letters as an entrée into an intriguing new world. She was fundamentally a realist and needed to think about her future. And so, with a few chance encounters
plus Keyserling's letters of introduction and Ortega's friendly squiring around
Paris, 1929, which had begun so unpropitiously, was to turn into a rewarding
year for Victoria.

Pierre Drieu la Rochelle

Less than a month after Keyserling left, Victoria met the writer Pierre Drieu la Rochelle at a small luncheon in Paris given in honor of Ortega. Other writers were there too, but it was the tall, blond, boyish Drieu with the enchanting smile who especially attracted Victoria. The feeling seemed mutual. Drieu wrote his wife that he had just met a beautiful foreigner and had fallen in love with her. A few days later Drieu baited Victoria with one of his books, a novel. She bit, and soon afterward they met for tea at Rumpel's. After that they spent long hours walking hand in hand along the streets and boulevards of Paris, going to the Louvre, to movies, to the opera, to the Comédie Française, and to his apartment on Isle Saint Louis.

As Victoria began to know Drieu she discovered his cynicism and his preoccupation with death and the decadence of Europe and America. He was moody, given to depression, and had "a taste for destruction that was like a hyena's for carrion" (A,5:52). Drieu had been a soldier in the world war and had some extreme ideas on war. For instance, he held that war evoked an ecstasy equal to that of Saint Teresa of Avila, or of women as they give birth. (Victoria later said she detested the derogatory way he portrayed women in his novels).

But Victoria began to notice her own rather perverse fascination with his twisted compliments: "You are the most beautiful cow on the pampa," and "you are like Lake Annecy, soft, abundant, clear water . . . where I can swim, extending all my members," and where, he added, he could "spit out his bitterness." (A,5:71–72) "Why then," she asked herself, "this idiotic tenderness and that sweet pleasure I felt in his company?" (A,5:83) Because, she said, he seemed like a lost child and brought out her maternal feelings of protectiveness—though she admitted that sometimes, as he rested his head on her shoulder, she would wish the guillotine for that head. Perhaps, too, because he was company for her at a time when she was a woman alone in a big city. "I accepted Drieu as a distraction from my preoccupations, as something deliciously removed from Keyserling" (A,5:72).

Her conversations with Drieu, Victoria said, revealed facets of life she had never before considered. She recognized in Drieu her own doubts about life, her feelings of unhappiness and emptiness as she was riding out the difficult, but critical, transition from passionate past to unknown future.

That winter of 1929 in Paris, Victoria, through Ortega, Keyserling, and Drieu, was introduced to a number of interesting people who were active in the cultural life of France. Among them were Paul Valéry, Benjamin Fondane, and Maurice Ravel. Most significant to Victoria's development as a feminist and

essayist were three women she met that winter: Anna de Noailles, Adrienne
Monnier, and Sylvia Beach.

Anna de Noailles

One of Keyserling's letters of introduction had been to Anna de Noailles, the
poet whom Victoria had read with such passion in her adolescence. Noailles
gave Victoria a warm welcome and soon the two women were seeing each other
almost daily.[12] Victoria wrote to Keyserling that she was charmed by Noailles,
amused by her flightiness and vanity, and won over by her enthusiasm and
her bubbling nature: "I like her just the way she is. It is so rare to find a being
as full of impulse as she is" (A,5:41).

But as Victoria came to know Noailles she saw that she was as antifeminist
in her views as the men of her times. Victoria was put off by her lack of solidarity with women, by her agreeing with Ortega that she and Sappho were the
only women poets in history worth noting, and by her taking as a hero Napoleon
(the author of the code that so limited a woman's world). For Victoria, an
idol of her youth had lost her charm. In the process, though, Victoria was forced
to face the disillusioning reality that not all writers are saints and not all women
writers promote the feminist cause.

Adrienne Monnier and Sylvia Beach

Güiraldes had once told Victoria that the next time she was in Paris she should
be sure to visit Adrienne Monnier in her bookstore, La Maison des Amis des
Livres, on the Left Bank. Going there in 1929, Victoria discovered a remarkable
woman who shared her own deep interest in books and writing.[13] For Monnier
not only had created a welcoming place for writers and intellectuals to meet;
she also ran a lending library, held readings, wrote essays, and in 1925 had
founded, directed, and paid for publishing twelve issues of a monthly review,
Navire d'Argent.

Monnier's dedication to the intellectual community of Paris and to her review were an inspiration to Victoria and had a significant influence on her when
the time came to start her own journal. But most importantly, Monnier had
a good friend across the street on rue de l'Odéon—Sylvia Beach, who ran the
bookstore Shakespeare and Company. Beach had the same warm receptiveness
to writers as Monnier, and besides that, she had a special enthusiasm for Virginia Woolf. It was Beach who gave Victoria a copy of Woolf's *A Room of One's
Own* and started Victoria reading the provocative works of the English feminist writer. For Victoria, Woolf's words were both an awakening and a tremendous reinforcement of many of the ideas she already held. Woolf would become

the person who most influenced Victoria's writing, giving her the courage and confidence, first, to persevere in her career as a writer, and then to use her own words to promote the cause of women—their education, expression, responsibilities, and rights. Sylvia Beach, by the simple act of handing Victoria a copy of *A Room of One's Own,* contributed immeasurably to Victoria's understanding of herself and feminism.

WALDO FRANK

As Victoria sailed away from Europe in 1929 to return to Argentina, she realized that, though painful, she must now find some other passion to fill the place of the love-passion she had known with Julian. Without knowing it, she was preparing herself to meet Waldo Frank, the next man to enter her life. He would have a profound influence on the launching of Victoria's career, not only as an essayist but also as a publisher. A writer of considerable reputation in the United States, Frank had come to Argentina in late 1929 as part of a Latin American lecture tour and Victoria first met him when he gave a talk on his friend, Charlie Chaplin.

> I liked him. I envied him because I couldn't talk the way he did. This meeting marks an important event in my life. My interest in the United States, its writers, its cities, its way of life, was suddenly aroused. (A,6:50–51)

Soon Frank was invited to Victoria's house, where they talked and talked. As she came to know Frank she realized that he was enamored of Latin America and of communism, though "much of Frank's communism was mystic and idealist."[14] Victoria also found that he was enamored of women in general— but apparently not of her. She said she felt only friendship for him and he seemed to respond in kind. She was not his muse; he was not her hero. No entangling complications this time. It was a friendship and synergy that grew out of a working relationship.

Victoria remembered Frank as sensitive, egotistical, and generous. She was particularly impressed because he was the first North American to take Argentina seriously: she felt it wasn't necessary for people to wrap themselves in gaudy ponchos to catch his attention. Victoria was fascinated as Frank dreamed aloud about a possible future where both Americas might be intellectually and spiritually united. She understood his pride in his own country, a pride tempered by feelings of discontent with a perceived materialism and loss of values, and she applauded his feverish interest in learning all about South America.

But Waldo Frank went even further. One afternoon walking in Palermo, Frank reproached Victoria for wasting her time and energies and essentially accused her of being a dilettante. He urged her to turn her talents to something serious, something worthwhile. And then he came out with the idea of starting a journal that would provide an intellectual link between North and South America.

To her surprise, Victoria took this well. Responding to Frank's enthusiastic insistence, Victoria was persuaded to try something she never dreamed she would do—found a literary magazine. This astounded her for she felt she was not prepared for such an endeavor. But, ready or not, before Frank left Buenos Aires she had promised to meet him in New York in 1930 and to start thinking of ways to turn his idea into a reality.

RETURN TO EUROPE

In the early spring of 1930 Victoria was once again in Europe. Among other things, she was hoping to test the reactions of her friends there to the idea of starting a literary journal in Argentina. She also wanted to see Drieu again. His ideas on women, Europe, and war might be abhorrent to her, but there was something appealing about him and she concluded that Drieu came as a package and that she would have to accept him as he was. They traveled to Germany together.

By chance, on her return to Paris from Berlin, she received a telegram from Tagore asking her to come visit him in southern France, where he had stopped off on his way to Oxford to give some lectures. Victoria wired back that she would love to see him. Before long she, her maid Fani, and her friend Delia del Carril (Güiraldes' sister-in-law) were driving down to the villa on Cape Martin, where Tagore was a house guest. She found Tagore totally absorbed in his new hobby, painting. When she suggested that she arrange an exhibit of his work in Paris, Tagore was as thrilled as "a teenager who wins some unexpected prize" (A,4:37).

On May 2, 1930, the exhibit of Tagore's paintings opened at the Galeria Pigalle, complete with a catalog for which Anna de Noailles had written the preface. The show was a success and went on to London and Berlin. The speed and efficiency with which Victoria had helped to organize things surprised and pleased everyone who knew her.

Warming to Victoria's return, Tagore asked her to accompany him to Oxford and then to continue on to India with him. Victoria was torn, but declined. She had promised Waldo Frank that she would come to New York and she felt she should keep her word. Victoria later confessed that the idea of traveling with Tagore seduced her not a little so that before she made her decision she went through a very bad time. But she continued to be ambitious, and going to New York and mapping plans for a literary journal were opportunities she did not want to miss.

Soon afterward, Victoria and Tagore parted forever at the Gard du Nord in Paris. A picture taken as they were waiting for the train shows them both looking distraught. Excerpts from her letter to Tagore in April of 1930 give a good indication of her frame of mind at this time.

> I must try to explain to you the reason or object of my travel to the USA . . . Waldo Frank (who is one of the few talented Americans feeling friendly toward South America) came to Buenos Aires and lectured there. I saw, through him, a new United States and an America of which I had never dreamt before. He saw through me a new America too. We were like a brother and a sister. . . . We were both orphans. Europe was the cause of that feeling.
>
> Our friendship is made of feelings and thoughts that go beyond ourselves. He was experiencing up north what I was suffering down south. And when we found that out, we were quite excited. This may sound childish, but I can't express it in better terms.
>
> We thought of making a bilingual magazine . . . Some people think it's foolish. Some, that it might be a fruitful experience.
>
> Waldo is studying South American history now, because he intends writing a book. He thinks I can be useful and wants to speak things over with me. I promised to go to see him in New York. I am very much troubled about it all, because I should like to stay with you in Europe.
>
> But if our magazine is going to be born, I feel it is necessary for me to talk matters over with Waldo and some of his friends. I believe Waldo's book on South America can be important. And I think our magazine could be important too.[15]

When, not long after Tagore's departure, Victoria sailed into New York, Waldo Frank was at the pier to meet her. He took her off to the Sherry Nether-lands, where from her window she could look down on Fifth Avenue and Central Park. She was enchanted by the skyscrapers, the Brooklyn Bridge, Harlem, jazz, and the strange jungle sounds rising from the Central Park Zoo at night—so much so that Frank became impatient. Victoria was spending more time exploring New York than she was pondering the problems of starting a literary journal.

Victoria was ambivalent, enthusiastic, but with doubts. As an eleven year old she had briefly "run" a magazine, with Angélica and Miss Ellis as collaborators. The urge to be an editor still captivated the almost forty-year-old Victoria.

> One is never cured of one's childhood. Once again I was being tempted by the idea of playing at publishing a magazine. But this time I realized the difficulties of the game and my own inadequacies. My passion for the written word . . . was not enough to guarantee the success of the proposed journal. (A,6:68–69)

She complained to Frank that she really did not know quite where to start. Where were all those young Argentine writers he kept telling her about?—those who needed a journal that would give them a rallying point and would publish their writing? She could help financially, but who would help her find collaborators?

Victoria kept enumerating the obstacles. One of the stumbling blocks was money; North American writers were paid so much and Victoria felt that it was unlikely that financial help for a literary magazine would be forthcoming in Buenos Aires. Frank came right back at her: "If you're not resolved to make sacrifices, to take this business seriously, let's not talk about it any further." To which Victoria replied: "I am resolved, but let me breathe and look around a little"(A,6:70).

So she looked around, and she listened. She walked around Greenwich Village, she went to the Cotton Club, she saw "Green Pastures," she listened to spirituals and gospel preachers. And she met Duke Ellington, Alfred Stieglitz, Lewis Mumford, and Sergei Eisenstein. It was a brief but stimulating introduction to New York. Nothing definite about the journal seems to have been decided, but by the time Victoria set sail for Argentina its seed had been sown.

Founding Sur

When Victoria returned to Buenos Aires in 1930 she was eager to found her literary review and to realize the dream of linking North and South America with Europe intellectually. Although several of her friends in Europe and Argentina were enthusiastic about her proposed journal, there were many negative voices in Buenos Aires. Her father told her quite frankly that she would go broke. Others declared that the notion of a journal was just the plaything of a woman who would soon tire of her toy. Still others added that the journal was doomed to failure because it was "the handiwork of a society lady who had gotten in way over her head" (SUR, 346:136).

Victoria thought she knew the problems she faced. She was fully aware of the disillusioning experiences of earlier Argentine journals—journals such as *Proa,* which had failed to survive its first year. But ambitious and tenacious, she now set out to make a success of her endeavor.

Fortunately, there were a few close friends to encourage and help her at this time. Foremost among them was Waldo Frank. Their dreams for the journal originated in different visions; Frank was concerned only with the Western Hemisphere, Victoria was firm on including Europe. In the end, Frank conceded that it should be *her* journal and thus she should be the one to determine its scope and to shape its future.

Ortega was another source of strong support. He had found Argentina materialistic and so absorbed in the economics of cattle and grain production that there was little time for reflection, but he also saw it as a young and vigorous nation with great potential. He urged Victoria to exert herself to develop her country in ideological and artistic areas, and he offered his own "meager powers" to help achieve that goal. A literary review concentrating on the arts and literature seemed ready-made for Ortega's enthusiasm and support. Ortega helped by contributing to the review and persuading other writers in Europe to do the same. When Victoria and her friends were unable to agree on a name for the review, Victoria picked up the phone and called Ortega in Spain. "Ortega didn't hesitate and among all the names I mentioned he immediately had a preference. '*Sur,*' he shouted at me from Madrid" (SUR,346:136). To the name *Sur,* Victoria added a trademark that would become famous: an arrow pointing south.

Victoria's willingness to undertake the job of starting the journal depended on a few friends in Buenos Aires who had agreed to help her and in whom she had confidence.[16] In addition, Victoria had a board of consulting editors that included Borges. The impressive list of foreign advisors to *Sur* reads like a capsule of her past: Ortega from Spain, Ansermet from Switzerland, Drieu from France, Frank from the United States, and Reyes from Mexico.

Sur was born in the Argentine summer of 1931. The first issue of four thousand copies quickly sold out in Buenos Aires, Madrid, and Paris. Reflecting the elite nature of the journal, the texts were accompanied by handsome illustrations and its two hundred pages were printed on high-quality paper by Francisco Colombo, who had produced Güiraldes' *Don Segundo Sombra.*

That first issue was a successful mixture of literature and the arts. There was an introductory note by Frank, an article by Borges on the Argentine writer Ascasubi, an essay by Ansermet on the problems of American composers, a letter to South American readers from Drieu, and an article by Gropius on his vision of the modern theater. There was also an essay on Picasso and one on Le Corbusier.

Sur became Latin America's foremost literary and cultural journal of the twentieth century and endured for over forty years. This was largely due to Victoria's determination, guiding influence, and infusion of money. (The "society lady" did not prove to be over her head.) With *Sur* Victoria had the chance to build the intellectual bridges she longed to construct and she also had a vehicle to express her own expanding ideas. It was not just Victoria's world that was growing larger now; through *Sur,* the outlook of many readers in Latin America was broadened to include glimpses of life and ideas far beyond Buenos Aires. Indeed, for Victoria, "the founding of *Sur* was the first step in leaving a lasting mark on Argentine culture."[17]

Illustrations

Villa Ocampo.

Victoria with her grandfather,
Manuel Anselmo Ocampo, in 1895.

Estancia "La Rabona"
Pergamino
1895

Victoria (smiling and with her feet to the camera) surrounded by Alejandro Leloir, Pancha Ocampo, Clara Ocampo, Saenz Valiente, Rosa Ocampo and Silvina Ocampo (holding a pet goat). At Villa Ocampo, about 1911.

Victoria at about seventeen.

Victoria in Paris, 1913.

Julian in Rome, 1913.

Victoria driving in Buenos Aires in 1922.

Victoria with Rabindranath Tagore in San Isidro in 1924.

Victoria at Mar del Plata in 1926.

Victoria with José Ortega y Gasset in Spain in 1930.

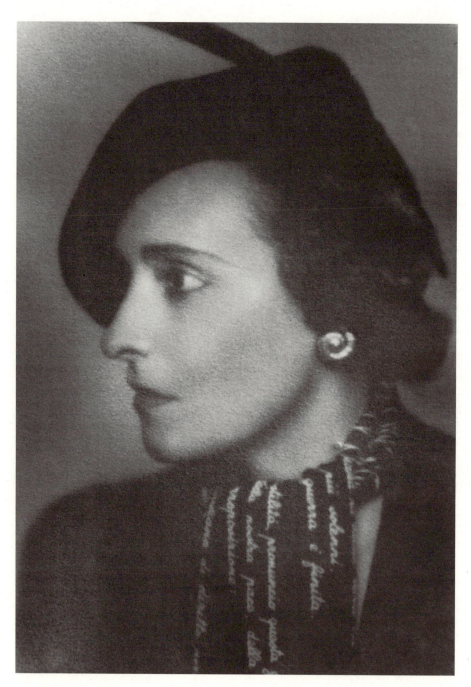

Victoria when she was about forty-five.

Victoria and André Malraux at Villa Ocampo in 1959.

Victoria in 1977 as a new member of the Argentine Academy of Letters.
(Photo by Pájaro y Fuego)

PART TWO

Life after Forty

(1931–1979)

Victoria's autobiography ends with the founding of *Sur*. After that, she said, her life was so closely bound to the review that *Sur*'s history was also hers. As the physical, emotional, and financial mainstay of the review, Victoria suddenly found that she was an entrepreneur with new responsibilities. Largely through her efforts, *Sur* became an elegant literary magazine with special emphasis on essays, but also featuring stories, poetry, the plastic arts, social commentary, and book and film reviews. John King described it as "one of the most important achievements in the cultural life of Latin America."[1]

Victoria at Forty

Victoria had come a long way in her first forty years. For the truth is that despite the disadvantages of being female in Argentina, despite the limited education of which she so liked to complain, despite her overly protective family and the stifling attitudes of her society, Victoria was well equipped to make her way in the world she found around her. She had been endowed with intelligence, great beauty, boundless energy, curiosity, enthusiasm, and a sense of humor. She could converse and read comfortably in several languages. She had ample financial resources to travel at will and, on occasion, to underwrite people and projects. And over the years Victoria was blessed with the presence of many people who influenced her at crucial turning points in her life. She seems to have been extremely fortunate in the way one person led her to another. It may have been her money or her beauty or her charm that attracted them initially, but in the end each of the important people who entered her life contributed in some way to her development as a woman and as a writer.

Victoria took an education that had been designed to prepare her for a circumscribed social world and used it to bring herself into a much wider, more stimulating world. She used the French, English, and Italian she had been taught as a girl for more than conversing with her dressmaker or her dinner partner. She put them to useful purpose by interviewing, lecturing, translating, and most significantly, writing. Instead of reading merely to amuse herself and while away the hours, she read voraciously and often commented in her essays on what she had read. As Beatriz Sarlo insightfully concludes: "What society considered an adornment, Victoria Ocampo transformed into an instrument."[2]

By making the most of everything she had been given and by accepting the help of friends she made along the way, Victoria finally succeeded in establishing her career. Founding *Sur* was a great achievement for Victoria and it proved to be the beginning of more than forty eventful and extremely productive years. During this time she not only became a literary and intellectual leader, but she also articulated her beliefs in writing, giving voice to her feminist convictions.

The First Years of Sur

Sur's first year was difficult. A military coup in Argentina in 1930 had set a pattern of cultural isolationism and intellectual suppression which naturally made *Sur* suspect. Beginning with the first issues, there was criticism of the review because of its international overtones and its decidedly elitist approach.

Not long after the founding of *Sur*, Victoria wrote to María de Maeztu that she was thoroughly depressed, adding, "You can't imagine how much I've struggled against the wind and the tide" (sur 303/305:11). When Victoria complained to Waldo Frank, he responded that *Sur* was fine and fresh, that she had to expect criticism, and that she should learn to shrug it off and persevere. He challenged her to accept the growing pains of the fledgling review and to be ready to grow herself.

Fortunately, Victoria had a strong sense of mission to sustain her during those first trying years. For she fervently believed in the aims she had stated in the first issue of *Sur:* that it should be a cultural bridge between the intellectual elite of the Western Hemisphere and Europe and that it should help to build a future literary elite in Latin America by encouraging young authors. She was determined to alert Europe and the United States to the best Latin American writers and to bring to Latin America the most outstanding works of Europe and the United States.

Committed to a high literary standard, Victoria declared that art does not allow for either equality or charity and that only talent should be rewarded. She sought out the ablest writers on the international scene and then found the best translators to bring their works to the Spanish readers of *Sur*. By encouraging young Latin American writers to publish in *Sur*, Victoria gave a start to many now famous men, most notably Jorge Luis Borges. Octavio Paz has spoken eloquently of Victoria and *Sur* as an intellectual and spiritual configuration of tremendous influence on the Latin American literary scene.[3]

Victoria was buoyed in establishing *Sur* by beliefs that had been a part of her since childhood and that now set the tone for the review. Basic to these beliefs was her recognition that it was natural to have an intellectual elite, that there should be free speech for everyone and an accompanying tolerance for diverse views. While Victoria always claimed that she was apolitical, she was also a strong advocate for democracy and opposed any form of totalitarianism. It is greatly to her credit that *Sur* kept publishing and maintained its civilized, liberal voice through the Spanish Civil War, through World War II, and through years and years of political turmoil in the Argentine government. Its last regular issue was published in 1970, when Victoria was eighty years old.

Problems

The growth and success of *Sur* for almost forty years should not minimize the problems in keeping it afloat, for there were many. Victoria had to deal with the usual trials and responsibilities of running a magazine: finding contributors, editing their works, meeting deadlines, cajoling advertisers, and trying to keep a variety of strong personalities happy and at peace.

In addition to that, from the beginning Victoria had to struggle against the pressures of the prevailing religious and political forces in Argentina. In July of 1935 she wrote Maeztu that "everything here is infected with lies, bad faith, ignorance, brutality, base ambition, vulgarity, and pompous prattle. . . . Peronism and clericalism keep pace with one another—it is a time of corruption running rampant."[4] The church took exception to her liberal views; they found her suspect, not only because of her less than spotless reputation, but because she entertained people (Tagore) who were enemies of the church and permitted Communists (Malraux) to write in *Sur*. Victoria was proclaimed *persona non grata* by a church she later described as embracing "the Catholicism of Pharisees" (A,6:63). The situation became even more difficult during Perón's dictatorship (1946–1955). Victoria was variously accused of being either a communist, a fascist, or a Nazi because she continued to publish the works of people of a great variety of viewpoints—people such as André Gide, Thomas Mann, T. S. Eliot, Martin Heidegger, Ezra Pound, André Malraux, Evelyn Waugh, Henry Miller, Albert Camus, Octavio Paz, and William Faulkner. Victoria proclaimed, but to little avail, that she simply published the works—not the ideologies—that appealed to her and that she had no interest in taking a political stance. But, interested or not, she was not immune to the political fray. In 1951 two crosses were painted on the gate to Villa Ocampo, a sign intended as a threat for Victoria and a warning to *Sur*. It was a warning that Victoria ignored.

Living in Peronist Argentina was like a bad dream. Early in the morning of May 8, 1953, the dream became a nightmare when six police agents came and took Victoria to a woman's prison in Buenos Aires, where she was held for twenty-six days.[5] Fortunately, and quickly, Victoria's imprisonment and the similar loss of freedom for many other intellectuals in Argentina became an international cause. Friends of Victoria's in New York organized the Committee for the Liberation of Argentine Intellectuals. *The New York Times* covered the situation closely, ran an editorial on Argentina's political situation entitled "Reign of Terror," and published Waldo Frank's strong letter decrying Perón's regime and pleading Victoria's case. Finally, through the passionate appeals of Gabriela Mistral, the Chilean poet, and the diplomatic efforts of Jawaharlal Nehru, then prime minister of India, Perón was persuaded to release Victoria. She was free in Argentina, but because her passport was confiscated she was unable to travel outside Argentina until Perón's overthrow in 1955.

Sur's finances presented yet another serious problem, for after two years it became clear that the review could not hold its own financially. Victoria had been personally underwriting it from the beginning, and though *Sur* had not been founded to make money, there was a limit to how much she could keep adding from her own resources. A partial solution was found in 1933, when Ortega persuaded Victoria to start a publishing house that would bring out Latin American works as well as books in translation—and hopefully bring in revenues that would help support *Sur.*

SUR

The addition of the publishing house, SUR, was an important step in Victoria's expanding career, for it meant that she oversaw the publishing of many fine Spanish and Latin American authors—Lorca, Borges, Mistral, Bioy Casares, Sábato, Onetti, Paz, Cortázar, and Vargas Llosa among them.

Perhaps the most significant product of SUR was its avid pursuit of books in Spanish translation. This brought to Latin American readers for the first time some of the most outstanding works being written in Europe and the United States. Early translations included *Point Counter Point* by Huxley, *Man's Fate* by Malraux, and *Psychological Types* by Jung. There followed, among many others, ground-breaking and sometimes controversial translations of the works of James Joyce, H. G. Wells, E. M. Forster, Vladimir Nabokov, Norman Mailer, and Jean-Paul Sartre. These translations were not only a boon for Latin American readers; they were also a tremendous stimulus to young Latin American writers and had a lasting impact on the development of Latin American literature.

Victoria took literary translation seriously. She recognized it as an art, as a re-creation, and as a valuable means of building cultural bridges. One of SUR's most significant contributions was to introduce Virginia Woolf to Latin American readers. *A Room of One's Own* and *Orlando,* both translated by Borges, were published in the 1930s, and *To the Lighthouse* and *Mrs. Dalloway* came a little later. Victoria herself translated several works that particularly appealed to her, among them works by Graham Greene, *Under Milk Wood* by Dylan Thomas, *Caligula* by Albert Camus, *Requiem for a Nun* by William Faulkner, and, with the help of the Anita Loos version, *Gigi* by Colette. Even at the end of her life Victoria's interest in translation continued. Ambitiously, in her eighties, she initiated a collection of world classics in translation, starting with a Spanish edition of *The Divine Comedy.*

Rewards

If the review, *Sur,* and the publishing house, SUR, created a seemingly un-ending series of problems for Victoria, they also brought her some remarkable rewards. First among those was that she came to know a wide range of interesting people whom she might never have met otherwise. She had a capacity for friendship, a flair for reaching out to new friends, often sending them books she had written, flowers (usually white orchids or roses), or even unique presents, such as the jar of molasses that sent Nancy Astor into grateful ecstasies, or the case of butterflies that both pleased and puzzled Virginia Woolf. Her friendships in Europe, Latin America, and the United States were sustained by literally volumes of letters.[6]

Travel had always been one of Victoria's great pleasures and *Sur* gave her an enhanced visibility and new opportunities; her travels now became enriched by the business of keeping in touch with writers and artists. In 1934 she and *Sur*'s editor, Eduardo Mallea, were invited by the Fascist Inter-University Institute of Culture to give a series of lectures in Italy. When Victoria responded that she had no sympathy with Mussolini's fascist government, her hosts insisted that she come anyway. It was a triumphant trip. As Victoria traveled through Italy, people marveled at her command of their language and hailed her as an intellectual ambassador from a young nation across the Atlantic.

While Victoria was in Rome she was asked whether she would like to meet Il Duce. Curious to see this rising leader, she said yes. (Most of the world, Victoria included, had not yet awakened to the threat of Mussolini.) On September 24, 1934, Victoria climbed the steps of the Palazzo Venezia and there, in a cavernous audience hall, while she sat and Mussolini stood over her, they spoke for almost an hour. She reported that they talked about literature, about Italy and its future, and especially about the condition of women in his country. She later recalled that Mussolini believed in the fertility of hate and not of love. She did not, of course, and told him so (E-6). As she was leaving, Victoria gave Mussolini a copy of *De Francisca a Beatrice* inscribed "To Benito Mussolini, the work of a student in search of her soul." When Mussolini asked whether she had found it, Victoria, undaunted, fired back that he shouldn't make fun of her.

From Italy, Victoria traveled to Zurich to visit Jung and get the rights to translate his *Psychological Types.* From there she went to London, where Aldous Huxley, whom she had met through Drieu, took her to the opening of an exhibition of the photographs by Man Ray, who had photographed Victoria in 1929. It was there, in that crowded room, that Huxley introduced her to Virginia Woolf. The two women were immediately intrigued by one another. Years later Victoria described this first meeting with Woolf.[7]

It was as if we had met on a desert island. She began a regular interrogation, quizzing me about apparently insignificant things. Were there many butterflies in Argentina? (This business of the butterflies fascinated her. I suppose she must have read in Darwin about the strange invasion of butterflies ten miles off the bay of San Blas.) She asked me what games I played when I was a little girl, how many sisters I had, what my house was like, what the countryside looked like, what impression I had of Mussolini. (T,9:42)

They became friends, and in the next few days Victoria went several times to Virginia's house on Tavistock Square, where they talked for hours about literature, about biographies, and, especially, about women. Virginia, the impressive feminist writer, was an inspiration to Victoria; Victoria, the exotic beauty from a distant land, fed Virginia's lively imagination. It was the beginning of an extremely fruitful relationship for Victoria, a relationship that would last until Virginia's suicide seven years later.

In the years to come Victoria often went back to visit friends in England, France, and Spain, and in 1943 she visited the United States once again. After World War II, at the invitation of the British Council, she went to Germany as an observer at the Nuremberg trials. To her regret, she never went to India though she was invited many times.

One of the tangible rewards that *Sur* and SUR gave Victoria was a place to publish, a place where, forever after, her writing would find a home. She took full advantage of this perquisite and published, literally, volumes. Indeed, *Sur* and SUR published more of Ocampo than of any other author. She confessed that the word "sprawling" could be applied to her works and that her *Testimonios* bore witness to her profligacy with words. She openly acknowledged that she tended to return to themes that especially interested her: her childhood, the conflicts women face, delight in nature, books and music. She added, however, that all writers, great or mediocre, are guilty of repetition and she stated quite firmly that she needed to repeat herself because her readers sometimes seemed not to get her message.

New Influences

In Victoria's later years there was a significant change in the people who influenced her. Earlier mentors like Ortega and Frank still had intermittent roles, but soon after the founding of *Sur* Victoria became attracted to a different set of people: Mohandas Gandhi, Gabriela Mistral, and Virginia Woolf. Each in his own way inspired or encouraged Victoria in her career.

GANDHI

The man who most influenced Victoria's growth as a person was Mohandas Gandhi. She had been impressed by the Gandhi she encountered in 1924 in his biography; seven years later, in Paris, she was overwhelmed by the flesh and blood Gandhi she heard speak on his interpretation of nonviolence. His words and his presence were memorable, although with his bare legs and sandals and his usual short white tunic, he did not make a very prepossessing appearance. And yet, despite his "physical insignificance," he communicated a spiritual energy that would remain with Victoria for the rest of her life.

> Gandhi spoke with extreme simplicity, without eloquence or the tricks of an orator. His voice never rose and its timbre, although very agreeable, lacked any special quality. His physical appearance . . . seemed scarcely suited to impress anyone, . . . scarcely designed to captivate a Parisian audience that was mocking by tradition and nature. . . . But, right before our eyes, that blasé audience was dominated, galvanized! (ss:64)

After his talk, Gandhi fielded a series of questions, some of them rather embarrassing, but Victoria reports that "unperturbed, he answered them all—fairly, sincerely, patiently—with a spiritual presence" that was impressive (ss:63).
Victoria was attracted to Gandhi for more than his philosophy of tolerance and nonviolence and his understanding of authentic love as love for one's fellow man. She saw his views on women as a welcome reenforcement of her

own deeply held beliefs. She liked his having said that "the wife is not the slave of her husband, but his companion and collaborator who shares equally in his times of happiness and suffering and who is as free as her husband to choose her own life" (T,8:189).

Gandhi demonstrated for Victoria the powerful effect of conviction transformed into action. He became for her the model who would be a guiding example of spiritual and moral courage.

VIRGINIA WOOLF

It was Woolf who especially encouraged Victoria in her career as a writer. Soon after they met, Victoria sent Woolf an essay she had written on Aldous Huxley. Woolf responded: "I'm so glad you write criticism not fiction. And I'm sure it is good criticism-clear and sharp, cut with a knife not pitch-forked. . . . I hope you will go on to Dante, and then to Victoria OKampo. Very few women yet have written truthful autobiographies. It is my favourite form of reading."[8]

In January, Woolf wrote Victoria to say that she liked the essay Victoria had written about her. (Apparently "Carta a Virginia Woolf" [Letter to Virginia Woolf] had been translated into English for the occasion) (E-4). "I don't usually like appearing as a private person in print, but on this occasion I can find no fault, and like what you say very much and thank you for it."[9] The following month Victoria sent Woolf a copy of the first volume of *Testimonios*. Woolf replied, "Your magnificent book has come. How tempting it is—I can't read a word of it, and yet every other word is almost one I know. I must wait for the French—or shall I begin to learn Spanish? . . . Thanks for the tantalizing Book."[10]

These responses were what Victoria had been longing to hear for many years and were a tremendous boost for her. Early in her friendship with Woolf she put her gratitude in writing: "If anyone in the world could give me the courage and hope to go on, it is you. You for being who you are and for thinking as you do."[11]

Besides feeling gratitude, Victoria was entertained by Woolf's fanciful perception of Argentina and even seemed to grasp with equanimity the slight tone of condescension in Woolf's perception of her.

Virginia spoke to me in her letters about our immense bluish green plains. "What do you call them?" She added in parenthesis, "They must be very impressive—like the wild cattle." And I thought as I read her: Holy God! With all the work it has cost our ranchers to breed cows, bulls, horses, sheep worthy of standing with the best of England. But if it amuses you to imagine things this way, Virginia, go ahead. Wild cattle, blue-green grasses on the pampa, butterflies whirling around in the air. Virginia created an Argentina to her own liking. (T,9:43)

"Every time I go out on the street" she wrote me, "I fashion another picture of South America. No doubt you'd be very surprised if you could see your house the way I imagine it and the way I have it all arranged. It's always hot and I see nocturnal butterflies on silvery flowers and all that in broad daylight."

It occurs to me that in the beginning Virginia felt a certain astonishment when she realized I could actually articulate with words. [For her] I was part of that Argentina of the wild cattle, the butterflies and the blue-green plains she had invented. She invented me too. (T,9:49)

Victoria saw Woolf just one more time, in 1939, before her suicide in 1941.[12] Virginia Woolf's influence on Victoria was enormous and complex. Woolf fulfilled Victoria's earlier need for hero worship, but she also provided a model, both as a woman and as a writer, to whom Victoria looked for guidance. She encouraged Victoria by reinforcing her ideas about women and stimulated her to think along new paths, especially the path that led her to write her autobiography. Perhaps most importantly, Woolf inspired Victoria to consider herself as a feminist, as one of many women in a long and worthy tradition.

GABRIELA MISTRAL

María de Maeztu introduced Victoria to the Chilean poet Gabriela Mistral in Madrid in 1930, but it was not until 1938, when Mistral stayed with Victoria in Mar del Plata, that the two women really became acquainted. There, walking in the garden or sitting on the beach, they talked and talked and became lasting friends. The extensive correspondence that sustained their friendship dates from this time.

They were an unlikely twosome. Their backgrounds and their ideas on women were at decided variance. Mistral was half-Indian and half-Basque, from a modest rural background; she did not share Victoria's liberal views on women. As Doris Meyer points out, they had almost contradictory personal modes: "Ocampo, an ardent feminist, had many love affairs and disdained the restrictions placed on women; Mistral, on the other hand, preferred the intimate company of women and believed that the politics of feminism would upset the social order."[13] They had little difficulty spotting each other's shortcomings: Mistral felt Victoria was too much of a Francophile and needed to express her Argentineness more, Victoria saw Mistral's concern for the Indians as bordering on fanaticism and disagreed with her belief that woman's place was in the home.

No doubt both their perspectives expanded tolerantly as they found some common ground and became lasting friends. Both were childless, both deeply attached to Latin America, and both crusaders, Mistral for native Indian rights, Victoria for the rights of women. And both were deeply committed to the education of women. Besides that, they were two intellectual women who shared the pleasure of talking together for hours, finding as much stimulation in discussing the spiritual aspects of life as they did in talking about literature.

Mistral's help was crucial to Victoria when she was imprisoned in 1953. Using her considerable influence, for she had been awarded the Nobel Prize for Literature in 1945, Mistral contacted friends in other countries, wrote articles alerting people in Europe and the Americas, and finally, she sent a cable to Perón pleading for Ocampo's release—and sent a copy as well to the Associated Press in New York.

Because Victoria's passport had been confiscated, she was unable to leave Argentina for two years. By the time she was able to travel to New York, her great friend was sick and beyond communication. Victoria felt her loss deeply: for years she had basked in the stimulation and warmth of Mistral's friendship, the protective caring of a passionate older "sister," and now she was gone.

Mistral, who Victoria later described as the most important Latin American woman of her time, supported and encouraged, chided and cajoled Victoria—always trying to help her achieve her best work. Victoria singled out both Gabriela Mistral and Virginia Woolf in her speech when she was admitted to the Argentine Academy of Letters in 1977. Her remark about them is significant: "I owe them something that has mattered in my life. . . . my not having been content just to exist" (E-21:23).

Honors

External rewards, for her years of directing *Sur* and SUR, began to come to Victoria in 1950 in the form of honors from around the world. There followed a succession of tributes, genuine recognition of her substantial contribution as an essayist and publisher. England, France, and India were lavish with their honors and in 1967 she received an honorary degree from Harvard.

Argentina also recognized her with an array of significant awards. Perhaps the honor closest to Victoria's now very old heart came in 1977, when she was given the Alberdi Chair in the Argentine Academy of Letters. As Doris Meyer recounts, "the public inside and outside the auditorium was eager to catch a glimpse of the woman who had been a queen of letters long before the Academy officially recognized her. Some of those who saw her, still tall and erect at eighty-seven, . . . were long-time admirers, people who had worked with her on *Sur,* friends or members of her large family. Others were more recent admirers, members of a younger generation who saw her as a pioneer in a golden age of Argentine letters, a venerable survivor of pre-Perón feminism, an aged but still legendary beauty" (DM:177). Victoria became the first woman ever to be admitted to this prestigious and, until then, exclusively male group of intellectuals. It was an honor for which, consciously or unconsciously, she had been striving for over fifty years.

Although her early rebellious nature might have made it predictable, Victoria was not born a feminist. As a pampered and protected girl, her interest was almost entirely in herself. Most of her time was spent among women—her mother, her aunts, her nursemaids, and governesses—who were comfortable with the status quo and had no inclination to initiate notions of women's liberation. In adolescence, as she began to feel the constraints of her circumscribed life, Victoria's rebellion took shape only in her thoughts, in her confidences to Marguerite Moreno, and in emotional letters to Delphina Bunge. The rebellion centered on her own plight and showed as yet no sense of being concerned with the problems of women more generally.

Early Feminist Models

It was reading that spurred her on as an emerging feminist. By the time Victoria was eighteen she was already familiar with the works of George Sand, George Eliot, and Elizabeth Barrett Browning. Victoria's first feminist model seems to have been Mme. de Staël. Victoria read and reread her novel, *Corinne,* later confessing: "More than ever I've had the impression of living what I read. I was Corinne. Her destiny was mine" (A,2:166). Victoria identified with the rebellious Mme. de Staël, who defended women's rights; she applauded the novelist's passion and honesty and she understood her statement that she wanted to express what was in her soul, much more than she wanted to create a work of art.

But in her early years Victoria appeared to be quite unaware of women writers of the Spanish-speaking world who might have sparked feminist ideas in her. She probably did not even know of the existence of the free-spirited feminist Gertrudis de Avellaneda (born in Cuba in 1814), who wrote so vehemently about slavery and the complex torments of love and marriage.[1] She surely did know of the popular poet and essayist Alfonsina Storni (1892–1938), whose works appeared regularly in *La Nación* as early as 1919.[2] But Storni's concerns were for shop girls and working-class immigrant women, her public was considered to be middlebrow, and Victoria paid her little or no attention and apparently kept her own social distance. Indeed, years later when Gabriela Mistral chided Victoria for ignoring Storni, Victoria replied rather curtly that they never had the chance to develop a friendship, nor did it occur to her to consider it indispensable.

Solidarity with Women

In 1926, after talking for days with Maeztu, Victoria began to realize that she might play a role in the struggle for women's rights. But she did not yet understand what that role might be. It was not until Victoria came to know Virginia Woolf, in 1934, that she became a declared feminist ready to put her convictions in writing. She observed how Woolf, through *A Room of One's Own,* had contributed to the struggle for women's liberation and she considered the constructive possibility of writing honestly, without rancor, for both men and women (as Woolf did). It was at that time, when she was in her mid-forties, that Victoria began to perceive herself in a progression of feminist writers, each in her own way chipping away at the problems of women's rights.

By 1936 Victoria was an active feminist. Fascism was spreading in Argentina and its impact on Argentine women was highlighted by the attempted reform of a law that would have completely wiped out the rights women had won in 1926. Under the proposed legislation, women would again become entirely dependent on their fathers, husbands, or sons. With her friends, María Rosa Oliver and Susana Larguía, she founded the Union of Argentine Women (UMA) in 1936; their primary goal was to bring together women of all social classes to fight the threatening reform.

As the Union gathered strength, its program expanded to call for not just the civil and political rights of women in general, but for the protection of women in industry, agriculture, and domestic service, for minors, and for mothers everywhere in Argentina. The UMA also called for an end to prostitution. The women held meetings, organized conferences, and carried their messages to the streets in leaflets, which they sold for a few pesos. One of the most popular of these pamphlets was Victoria's essay "Women, Her Rights and Her Responsibilities," written in June of 1936. In it, she proclaimed that the liberation of women would have a tremendous impact worldwide and that women themselves must take the initiative to bring an end to men's mistreatment of women, whether legal, physical, or verbal (E-7).

Victoria's insights were broadened by the ideas she found in books such as J. S. Mill's *The Subjection of Women* and Havelock Ellis's *Studies in the Psychology of Sex.* These liberal works, as well as others as diverse as books by Henrik Ibsen, Carl Jung, D. H. Lawrence, and André Malraux, greatly influenced her thinking about women and subsequently helped shape her essays.

Over the years Victoria gradually enlarged her focus to include women from many parts of the world. She had long been aware of women's struggles in the United States and Britain, but through the visibility given to them by the United Nations, Victoria began to express concern for women in distant countries like Russia and China, Australia and Iraq. By the 1950s, realizing that the campaign for women's rights was far from ended, she concluded that the UN was ideally positioned to carry on the struggle. In 1952, together with Eleanor Roosevelt and other prominent women, she went to Ireland to attend the UN Convention on the Political Rights of Women. The very fact that the convention was being held, she proclaimed, symbolized the progress achieved by women in the past century. Victoria was later to become temporarily disillusioned about the direction that the UN was taking on women's issues, but that did not keep her from her overall commitment to the world organization.

One event in her life particularly deepened her understanding of community with women: her incarceration in Buen Pastor prison in 1953. For twenty-six days she shared a room with eleven women prisoners of varying ages and economic and social backgrounds. That intensive experience was, she later realized, a blessing in disguise, a time of spiritual growth.

> I learned the meaning of the word solidarity among very diverse human beings. We were a group of women with different jobs, coming from different social environments and accustomed to different ways of living. . . . Never before have I known such a sense of well-being—something like happiness, something that almost canceled out our feeling of despondency. . . . This living together for a month under disagreeable conditions . . . revealed to me the immense possibilities for understanding and fraternity among people who might seem to have little in common. (E-13:241)

In the 1960s Victoria became aware of the dizzying pace of the women's revolution in the United States. She read Betty Friedan's *Feminine Mystique* and Robin Morgan's *Sisterhood Is Powerful*. She became familiar with the ideas of Gloria Steinem, Angela Davis, and Marya Mannes. Although she rejected extreme feminist positions, especially any resort to violence, Victoria continued to have an interest in the concerns of women right up to the time of her death.

When Victoria was eighty-five, she met Susan Sontag in Paris and recognized her as she might a daughter, the incarnation of her own unrealized dreams. She did not agree with all of Sontag's ideas, but she could understand how Sontag had come to them, and she respected her. Being able to empathize with a radical feminist perhaps forty-five years her junior was a special mark of Victoria's feminism and a measure of the sense of community that exists among women of all ages.

Broadening Perspectives

While Victoria was developing as a feminist she was, of course, also growing as a person. By 1935 both her mother and father had died. Saddening though this might have been, it was liberating: her years of anguish for fear of offending her parents by her actions or words were now over. The psychic energy involved in this preoccupation could be spent on other concerns.

From Tagore and Gandhi and the teachings of the New Testament, Victoria had come to internalize the universal truth that all men are brothers. Glimpses of this perception are apparent in her account of the burial of her friend Ricardo Güiraldes, in 1928.

No longer living, he returned from his last trip to Europe. His friends went to wait for him at the pier as we had done other times. And we went along with him then as far as a small, simple cemetery near his ranch in San Antonio de Areco, very far from the city, on the edge of that pampa which was his favorite place.

. . . Waiting for us at the station, in the middle of a field, was a group of gauchos on horseback dressed in their finest clothes; *chiripa,* baggy trousers, knotted kerchiefs, wide belts gleaming with silver, whips in hand, and on their heads narrow-brimmed hats. They had been friends to Ricardo and he had loved them like brothers. My eyes searched theirs for a feeling similar to mine. . . .

They accompanied us in silence as far as the cemetery. There were gauchos covering the pampas for as far as we could see . . . Watching them disperse, after it was all over, I thought about *Don Segundo Sombra.* I had just seen the last page of Güiraldes's novel of the pampa performed before my very eyes. Those men, now scattered, had said good-by to Ricardo as the young Fabio Cáceres said good-by to Don Segundo. . . . The gauchos departed without any show of emotion, just as they had come. Nothing was more moving than their silence. (T,2:324–26)

An experience in England in 1938 led her to express her sense of spiritual unity with all of humanity. It happened one September afternoon as the Munich crisis was reaching its climax and the Big Four powers were deciding the fate of Czechoslovakia—and Europe. Victoria, feeling the need of consolation, took refuge in London's national cathedral and later gave a talk, in English, about her experience there.

> The bells of Westminster Abbey, indifferent to our anxious waiting, struck a quarter past six, as usual with the peaceful, invariable accent of my distant Retiro. . . . Many, like us, had chosen that refuge to pray, wait, despair, be silent. We felt linked to those strangers by the same fixed idea. We looked at each other realizing that, without knowing one another, we had chosen that meeting ground and that we recognized each other at that sign. It was as if we leaned on one another without knowing who offered support and who looked for it. This mutual support, this sense of fraternity, surged up almost independently of ourselves and yet it embraced us, encompassed us. . . . This was, in truth, human solidarity. (T,2:511–12)

Victoria's first written acknowledgment of her conviction that all men are brothers came in 1941: "We are all made of the same substance. So close to one another without knowing it, without on occasion accepting it. United by our common human condition" (E-9:419).

Putting her growing sense of brotherhood into action, Victoria extended her generous hospitality to exiles from Spain during the Spanish Civil War. Later, in World War II she not only helped organize the shipment of three tons of food and clothing to Paris, to be distributed by Adrienne Monnier, but she personally welcomed several refugees, most notably the photographer Gisèle Freund.

Years later, listening to a speech by Josephine Baker, Victoria was intrigued when someone asked the black singer about her multilingual, multicolored adopted children and whether her experiment had been a good one. Victoria's comment on Baker confirms her growing belief in a world without barriers. "Ms. Baker answered that for her there was no other race than the human race and that her children got along very well. I very much like her language and I like her way of thinking" (T,8:302). In 1969, fascinated by the early lunar flights, Victoria went even further:

> One of the great advantages of those journeys into outer space is that the day will come when man will be obliged to speak as Socrates did. When they asked the Greek where he came from he didn't say "From Athens." He answered, "From the world." (T,8:195)

Relationship to Men

Part of Victoria's sense of solidarity with humankind is shown in her relationship to men, which is important to understand in order to fully comprehend her feminism. What makes Victoria different from many feminists is that she did not consider men the enemy. Though she spared no ink in denouncing the patriarchal suppression of women, her feminism embraced a tolerant, constructive understanding of life.

Victoria liked men and knew that they could be quite wonderful as heroes or mentors, friends or lovers. But this did not blind her to the problems of men or marriage. Indeed, she chided men for being insensitive, childish, and hopelessly set in their ways; she often exposed their easy resort to the double standard; and she was unrelenting in her criticism of men for propelling the world into so many wars.

In her feminism, as in her views of men, Victoria was both a realist and an idealist. She knew that men are strong and are here to stay, and yet she wanted to find a way to live with them—on an equal footing. But she wanted more than coexistence with men: she hoped that men and women might be joined in an equal, but complementary, partnership based on love and respect. And she looked forward to a time when women, rather than replacing men as leaders, would be educated to take their own rightful places, beside men, as equals.

PART THREE

Ocampo's Essays on Women

(1920–1977)

In 1931, when Victoria was articulating the aims for *Sur,* her interest was only in an international literary exchange. She did not single out any desire to write on issues of special interest to women. It was not until 1934, when she met Virginia Woolf, that Victoria became conscious of herself as a feminist writer. From then on she declared that she wanted to write as a woman, not by imitating male writers, but by speaking in her own voice from her own perspective.

> My only ambition is to some day manage to write, more or less well, more or less badly, but as a woman. If I had a marvelous lamp like Aladdin's and by rubbing it I was able to write like a Shakespeare, a Dante, a Goethe, a Cervantes, or a Dostoyevsky, it occurs to me that I would throw away the lamp. Because I think that a woman cannot express her feelings and thoughts the way a man would, no more than she can speak with a man's voice.
>
> . . . I am as convinced as you are that a woman does not really succeed in writing like a woman until she abandons that preoccupation with bitterness, until the moment when her works, no longer veiled responses to attacks that may or may not be veiled, have only to translate her own thoughts, feelings and visions. (E-4:12,15)

In this essay, an open letter to Virginia Woolf, Victoria acknowledged that she was a little overzealous when it came to women: "Whenever the occasion arises (and if it doesn't arise I go looking for it), I declare my solidarity with women." She quickly learned to counterpunch by taking an argument that might have little or nothing to do with women's issues and changing the focus so that she could inject her own ideas about women. An example of this is her exchange of letters with José Bergamin, a Spanish writer sympathetic to the Republicans in the Spanish Civil War. Calling Victoria "an enemy of Spain," Bergamin accused her in no uncertain language of dishonoring herself and betraying "her moral responsibility as the editor of *Sur*" by offering hospitality, "out of an apparent false, quixotic generosity," to "the renegade" Gregorio Marañón.

Printing his letter, and her reply, in *Sur,* Victoria deflected and then elevated Bergamin's attack to a new and different level.[1] She agreed that she had a great moral responsibility, but perceived it as her responsibility as a woman who felt she must answer for her actions and words. She asserted that like women everywhere who are accustomed to giving life, not death, she was horrified by wars and revolutions. She announced that her primary concern was for the proletariat of women, not for the proletariat of workers. She continued by asking Bergamin if he had ever considered an even more hateful exploitation than that of the Spanish workers—men's humiliating suppression and exploitation of women. Then she further diverted Bergamin's attack by suggesting that he should not just think of Spain but should go out into the world and try to experience a kind of human fraternity that, at its best, knows no frontiers.

Victoria used digressions to expound her views on women, no matter what the situation being discussed. This happened, for example, in her essay "Impressions of Nuremberg," with her reflections on the trials of Nazi war criminals to which the British Council had invited her as an observer. On the small Dakota flying from Croydon, England, to Germany in 1946, Victoria recorded that she was the only woman in a small group of mostly military men. One look at the toilet aboard the Dakota convinced her that the plane had been designed with only men in mind. Again, at the International Military Tribunal, she observed that there was not a woman in sight.

This tribunal, that airplane, did not foresee taking women aboard. The two had been constructed and organized with the intention of leaving them out. Women, it would seem, have no place in the masculine sport of war whose consequences they have to endure.

Hitler's business has been men's business. There are no women among the accused. Is that why there are no women among the judges? Wouldn't that be a better reason to include women? If the outcome of the Nuremberg process is crucial to Europe's destiny, wouldn't it be an act of justice for women to have some say in it? . . . Are women unfit to make decisions that will weigh on the future of the world? Until now the utter failure of men when it comes to the repression or prevention of the crimes of war and, indeed, of war itself—which is always a crime—has been a resounding failure. (E-11:53)

Style

Victoria had no illusions about writing great literature; her aim—indeed, what she understood as her "literary destiny"—was only to express herself and communicate her ideas. In writing her essays, Victoria first established a direct, personal relationship with her audience. She addressed her reader, whether male or female, as an intelligent person whom she assumed was part of a well-informed intellectual elite. Sprinkling her essays with French words and often taking her themes from texts by, for example, Proust, Shakespeare, Bertrand Russell, or Dwight Macdonald and enhancing her arguments with literary quotations, she was demanding of her readers.

Victoria's style is by turns serious, imaginative, lyrical, passionate, and theatrical. She is conversational, frequently confessional, and sometimes a little self-deprecating. Occasionally she is given to wild exaggeration, as in a statement about the red tape that besets women who want to pursue a career: "I know from hard experience, which I have survived, like those who have escaped from a concentration camp" (T,9:227).

One of Victoria's strengths was her use of metaphors. A notable example, cited earlier (on page 55), was her characterization of the commentators on Dante. But there are many others, such as describing Colette's French "as juicy and perfect as ripe fruit," and that hearing Mistral speak of her continent was "to hear a branch blossom." Victoria's essays are lightened by occasional touches of humor, whether of a passing playfulness or with the biting edge of her sarcasm or irony. It is, of course, her own unique style, feminist or not, honest and intense, but never strident.

From time to time Victoria apologized for "the inadequacy" of her style; her apologies seem sincere, not a stylistic carryover from the old Spanish formula where the author began his work by prostrating himself before his own unworthiness. Frustrated at times because she felt that people did not fully grasp what she was trying to say, she tended to repeat her most important ideas. But whatever her misgivings about her abilities as a writer, she managed to find a style that satisfied her and that conveyed her feminist message for over five decades.

Subjects

Inspired by her own experiences and her reading, Victoria wrote volumes of essays. She put into practice Woolf's message in *A Room of One's Own* that women should express themselves in writing, being barred from no subject, however trivial or vast. Of these many, many essays I consider her feminist essays to be of the most enduring interest; they seem to fulfill the purpose for which so much of her life had been preparing her.

EDUCATION

Victoria's voice was confident and her beliefs firm as, from essay to essay, she expounded on the subject of the education of women. In an article in *La Prensa* in 1947, she exhorted Argentine women to educate themselves.

> . . . The education of women is, in my judgment, one of the impera-tives of our times, since the future depends on women. We must not spare any efforts in seeing that this so neglected education is improved and com-pleted.
>
> . . . I say to you, Argentine women, that this is a grave moment; let us ed-ucate ourselves, instruct ourselves, impose disciplines on ourselves, so that we will be able to act effectively when the less imperfect order that we have helped to put in place has finally been established in this world.
>
> Let us prepare ourselves to form part of the "elite" (I am not afraid of the word) that will rule our destinies. It will not be an elite of birth, nor of money, nor of brute force. (E-16:174–75)

EQUAL RIGHTS

Victoria's essays reflect her unwavering commitment to the struggle for equal rights for women. She believed that the revolution to emancipate women was of paramount importance to the world and would have tremendous reper-cussions on the future—greater even than the Industrial Revolution. As early as 1936, in her essay "Woman, Her Rights and Her Responsibilities," she urged women to abandon their often too easy submission to men and to take their places in "the first line of the trenches." She saw the battle as having two great justifications: to liberate women from the yoke of patriarchal societies and to bring about peace among nations. Here the woman's role was key: she must be educated so that she could become responsible for her own life and assume an intelligent role in society. For, she declared, "rights are inseparable from responsibilities" (E-7).

In her essay "Woman's Past and Present," written in 1966, Victoria expressed her basic tenet this way: "For centuries half of humanity has been deprived of the most elemental rights of self-determination without causing the blink of an eye. Where was the male sense of justice? The female sense of dignity?" (E-14:236)

By 1969 Victoria had vested many of her hopes for women in the United Na-tions. Commenting on the *Universal Declaration of Human Rights,* she wrote that the fact that all men and women should be equal is "a truth that, for all the forms it takes, is one, indivisible. A truth for all Continents, for all races, for all times" (T,8:187).

In this essay, she said that she was further encouraged by the declaration of the United Nations advocating the elimination of all forms of discrimination against women. The United Nations focused on countries where women were not allowed to vote, to hold public office, to own property, to choose their own careers, or even to choose their own husbands—and, of course, where women had no possibility of enjoying the benefits of equal pay for equal work.

At eighty-two, Victoria was still writing vigorously, still pleading the cause of women's rights. "I believe that there are a good number of us who dare to declare that we are feminists and that feminism is nothing more than being conscious, as a woman, of the oppression than women have endured and still endure. Economic, judicial, sexual and psychological oppression" (E-16:172).

In 1975, at the Congress for the International Year of the Woman in Paris, Victoria became critical of the United Nations when she discovered that high on the agenda of the women's conference would be discussions centering on the rights of nations to self-determination and the struggle against colonialism and foreign domination. She registered her disapproval in an essay whose title in English would be "Words that Won't Succeed in Being Read at the Conference for the International Year of the Woman (E-20)." She protested that it was a disservice to women to introduce such diversionary concerns when flagrant injustice to women still existed. And, she added:

> I don't understand how these topics are linked to the specific demands of women. They seem far from the principal points that need to be resolved and that, shamefully, are not even mentioned. This present set of topics should be entertained by a Congress for the International Year of Men and Politics. . . . Frankly I don't think we will advance our cause by following this route. Before helping men to resolve problems of their own planting, women have to try to find solutions to their own problems and, united, without frontiers, not giving ground for any motive or pressure. . . . If we women do not solve our own problems, no one will solve them. (E-20:277–78)

VOTING RIGHTS, SUFFRAGETTES, AND ANTIFEMINISTS

Although she had long supported equal voting rights for women in Argentina, Victoria made little mention of this in her essays. Rather, it was the British suffragists who early captured her imagination and became a focus in many of her essays. She often mentioned Mrs. Pankhurst, the English suffragist, in passing and exhorted modern women never to forget the debt they owed to the early suffragists, known or unknown, who had cleared the way for later generations of women.

For Victoria, privileged women who committed the unpardonable sin of being indifferent to the struggle for women's rights were reprehensible. An example was her namesake, Queen Victoria. Again and again in Ocampo's essays, the queen was excoriated because she had so much power but would not use it to promote women's rights. Victoria singled out women like Anna de Noailles, who opposed the emancipation of her own sex, and who, Victoria claimed, expounded on the subject with more vehemence than the severest of Victorian fathers. One of the things that really galled Victoria was that Noailles's favorite hero was Napoleon.

> Only an antifeminist could have a predilection for the Bonaparte who was responsible for a Civil Code in which the incapacity of women was established in so many areas. According to this code, a woman can not inherit, sell, travel, study for a profession, etc., without the authorization of her husband. And worse: this code prohibits any investigation of paternity. . . . Strange legislation for a country that with drums, cymbals, and plenty of blood had just proclaimed "liberty, equality and fraternity" as their only ideal. (E-14:236)

When women's suffrage was finally won in Argentina in 1947, during Perón's harsh dictatorship, Victoria opposed the new legislation because it had been accomplished for purely political reasons by a corrupt fascist regime. In her essay "La trastienda de la historia" (The Backroom of History), written years after all of this had happened, Victoria tried to explain her position.

> When, in this part of America, the vote was given to women belatedly, it was much more like a male maneuver, like loyalty to a political party, than like the result of revindicated thirst, a thirst for justice, on the part of women. Mrs. Perón says so in *La razón de mi vida* [*My Mission in Life*], on page 262: "I recognize," she writes, "above all, that I began working in the feminist movement because Perón's cause demanded it."
> . . . Our cause was not that of some male politician, or of some political party. . . . It was a cause that was purely and exclusively concerned with the rights of women. Our negative response to granting the vote in 1947 was

not a reaction to political antagonisms, but rather to the reasons for which the vote was given. The vote was awarded for purely political motives and not to benefit our cause, that of all women. (E-15:229–30)

INTELLECTUAL CAPACITY

Victoria believed in the intellectual potential of women. It was vitally important to Victoria that women be seen as having the capacity for intellectual achievement; she longed for this recognition, not just for herself, but for women in general. Although well aware that a woman's beauty could be a valuable asset, she cautioned that no woman could trade on her beauty without prostituting herself. Instead, she urged women to get the best education possible and to have a career, if that was their choice. In short, women should use their brains, speak for themselves, and let their influence reach beyond their living rooms.

Victoria expressed these beliefs in her response to the epilogue that Ortega had, to her astonishment, appended to *De Francisca a Beatrice.* She took exception to his views of women, which could be summed up by the phrase "Man acts; woman merely exists." Although Ortega was courtly, even seductive, in his praise for Victoria's long essay on Dante, he showed little intellectual interest in her book. Instead, he revealed his attraction to Victoria and her magical powers as a muse. ("You, Señora, are an exemplary apparition of femininity . . . with a heart that is a nest of perfect enthusiasms and vigorous disdains") [FB:92]). For Ortega assigned women a passive role in life where, except for the casual gestures of her hand, she does not move. Her brain does not move much either. She communicates through her eyes and her smile and her charm. Indeed, as a re-creation of *amor cortés,* she is "as calm as the rose on the rose bush" (FB:108).

Clearly, as Ortega pictured it, "the active life is not the destiny of women." She leaves science, art, politics, and battles to the men. Her strength is not in *knowing,* but in *feeling,* for "to know things is to deal in concepts and definitions and that is the work of man." As for woman, "her job is to be the concrete ideal for men. Nothing more, but nothing less." Woman's destiny lies in trying to make herself "more perfect, more delicate" and more exacting in her demands on men to be more perfect. It was as an inspiration for men's deeds that Ortega believed women would have some influence on history; surely not, he protested, by the route that modern feminism would like to lead them. "It is incredible that there are minds so blind as to say that women can influence history as much by having the vote or a university degree as she does by the magical potential of illusion" (FB:105, 108, 101, 102).

Victoria's response to Ortega is measured. She does not directly attack him in ways we might have expected. Instead, she shows him, chapter and verse, that women can use their minds, that they read actively, and that through the written word they might even have a little influence. She shows but does not "tell" Ortega that she has an active brain. She wrestles with such weighty matters as "the crisis of our time," the relationship of the body and the soul, and definitions of happiness and love. She discusses the ideas of Bertrand Russell and Teilhard de Chardin and uses as examples such works as Shakespeare's *Othello,* Lawrence's *Lady Chatterley's Lover,* and Colette's *Cheri* (E-3).

SEXUAL NATURE OF WOMEN

As a young woman Victoria's ideas on sex, like her beliefs on many other subjects, were ahead of her times. But it was not until late in her life that she wrote directly on women and sex, and not until after her death, when her autobiography was published, that the sexual Victoria was revealed. The delay was her solution to the dilemma of being determined to tell the unvarnished truth about her early life, while not challenging the rigid standards of feminine propriety which included the taboo against a woman writing about her own body, or even worse, adorning her reminiscences with descriptive details about her sexual life.

In her 1954 book *Virginia Woolf en su diario,* Victoria launched into André Gide's thoughts about women's sexual nature and his strange "marriage blanc" to his cousin, Madeleine.[2] Victoria followed her comments on Gide with an outspoken discussion of her own beliefs about sex.

Gide, "a man of great intelligence," had openly admitted, in his journal, his ignorance in believing that only men felt sexual desire. Perhaps women of bad reputation had similar feelings, but surely not the admirable women of his childhood. It would have been insulting to these models of decency and honor and modesty to suspect them of any stirrings of the flesh. Gide's words were too much for Victoria.

> For Gide then, the models of decency, of honesty, of modesty, possessed such virtues only because their senses were dulled, not because they resisted temptation. Strange vision and strange moral in Gide. He believed, therefore, that the decency, the honesty, and the modesty of women depend exclusively on a deficiency or on a physiological abnormality that finds its label in medicine: frigidity. He also believed that that deficiency constituted her most precious attribute and that it was found among "respectable" women:

mothers, aunts, sisters (perhaps even cousins). According to Gide, women of ill repute were born by parthenogenesis and, therefore, were not able to boast of any kind of kinship bonds.

Referring to the female "colony" in human society (and I use the word *colony* as it is used to designate that of beavers and other small animals), Gide observes that biological laws exist that are quite similar to those of the bee-hive: fertile queen on one side, neutral female worker on the other. Naturally, the male drone escapes all sexual classification which might relegate him to a lower level yet, thereby limiting his supreme sexual independence. The comparison between human beings and bees only applies to women. Men, created in the image and likeness of God, should not, of course, compare themselves to an animal whose sexual life responds to the seasons.

On the other hand, women, born from a simple rib and twelve times impure while the earth makes its revolution around the sun, are closer to nature, men say with assurance. And nature is wise, they add, when it deals with imposing limits on the independence of women. Men then go on to explain why, given that physiologically women are weak, etc., it is necessary that they resign themselves to a lower level of life, etc.

It is important to emphasize that such a flexible argument taken from nature can be stretched in any direction and that men use it to defend the most contradictory justifications and the most absurd positions . . . when it suits their purposes. Gide uses this rationalization quite freely to make homosexuality seem as natural as heterosexuality, or even more so. For him, Nature serves to explain it all, according to the palate of each person. (vw:44–47)

In support of her outrage with Gide, Victoria cited Havelock Ellis, whose insights about sexual responsiveness in women were explicated in his authoritative *Studies in the Psychology of Sex*. Victoria agreed with Ellis's opinion that it was an unadulterated bit of foolishness to think that only lascivious women find pleasure in the connubial embrace.

Victoria was all for women expressing their sexual natures, but she was strongly opposed to de-eroticized love or anonymous sex where the partner is only an object. In 1931, in her reply to Ortega, Victoria cited Lady Chatterley as an example of a person who had replaced "love" by the word "sex." "Sex is for her something that has the importance of a cocktail" (E-3:204). She represented, Victoria asserted, one of the great problems of this century, the disassociation of love from the act of sex.

In the Middle Ages it was the soul that wanted to be separated from the body and to live on its own. The body is what people wanted to negate. But today it is the body that fights back by breaking away from the soul; the soul is what people want to negate. . . . I am talking about the younger generation, an international, intellectual elite who only see the body as a machine that dispenses the pleasant and the unpleasant; a machine which, consequently, has great importance and needs careful tending. (E-3:206)

MARRIAGE AND THE FAMILY

Victoria was opposed to marriages of convenience, which she equated to prostitution. She also felt that women should have the important right to terminate their marriages with a legal divorce. After her own disastrous marriage, she apparently never felt tempted to try it again. In fact, Victoria seemed to have been afraid of marriage, afraid that "its atmosphere of a warm greenhouse that protects happiness from the winds of the spirit" might breed sterility. She recalled a time in Paris, in 1929, when she had gone to a hotel to visit a friend who was on her honeymoon. As Victoria entered the couple's room, she found their luggage in disarray, the bed unmade.

My two little turtledoves held each other gently. The breakfast tray with their two cups was waiting for them on the table. There was something there of encirclement . . . materially and spiritually, that gave me a furious attack of claustrophobia. I remember leaving the room like someone drowning and then striding up the Champs-Elysées, breathing the cold air with delight . . . and thinking . . ."What a prison that room is!" (A,5:20)

Victoria's ideal, though she never found it for herself, was marriage based on mutual love and respect, "the magnificent union of two equal beings who mutually enrich one another since they possess different wealths." A union that can only exist between those who are ready to lay down their arms and fully accept their interdependence (E-7:264).

Because women have the prime responsibility for bringing up their children, and hence for the shaping of a future generation, Victoria gave mothers an esteemed place in her view of the family:

. . . the hope of the world is in our hands; it is entrusted to our care, to our loving care. But be careful, this hope of the world, the child, will be what we women ourselves are and not what we wish he might be. For we women are either an example for him or we are nothing.

Holding up the example of Mme. Curie who took her young children with her to the laboratory, Victoria was hopeful that women would find successful ways to combine their marriages with careers. For she warned that it was not healthy for women to try to satisfy their needs by living through either their husbands or their children.

> A woman, just like a man, can be a variety of things, all at one time; muse, artist, scientist, wife and mother. Motherhood, like religious orders, may require a woman to consecrate herself to it, and to forgo other concerns for a period of time, but it is not sufficient to fill the life of a woman who has desires of another kind; intellectual curiosity, artistic leanings, etc. Once she is free of having to care for her children (and in our day that happens quickly) what will she do with her time, no matter how much of a housewife she may be? (A,5:16)

SINGLE MOTHERS AND ILLEGITIMATE CHILDREN

Victoria was sympathetic to single mothers and felt there should be no discrimination against them or their illegitimate children, that they should be given the same rights as "legitimate" mothers and children. In "Pepita," Victoria wrote about the disgraceful experience of Vita Sackville-West's grandmother, Pepita, who fell in love with the British diplomat Lionel Sackville-West, and subsequently gave birth to an illegitimate daughter whose record of birth announced that she was born of "an unknown father." Pepita was ostracized from society and excommunicated from the church, and the little girl, Vita's mother, was treated as "a poor bastard child." Victoria concluded that, once again, there was a punishing double standard at work—men escape, women bear society's scorn (E-17:151–52).

SEXUAL HARASSMENT AND RAPE

Victoria opposed sexual harassment in its many forms, but she was careful to point out that we must be on the alert to the dangers of overzealous, and perhaps false, accusations that could ruin a man's career (E-18).

Near the end of her life, Victoria wrote about rape, calling it a crime for which the perpetrators should be put in a cage in the zoo. In an essay written in her eighty-sixth year, she expressed her agreement with the words of the American feminist, Angela Davis: "the leniency that men show toward rape, if it doesn't happen to their daughter or their wife, comes from being tied to the social and political function that grants supremacy to the man" (E-19:45).

On a more personal level, Victoria rose to Keyserling's accusation, in his book *South American Meditations,* that down deep Latin American women, presumably including Victoria, wanted to be violated and that men exercised the violation as a very natural thing. Such an accusation, Victoria protested, was "not something that I can let pass without a reply." She ended the matter by declaring that the "most brilliant answer" to Keyserling was Susan Brownmiller's book on rape, *Against Our Will* (T,10:71).

BIRTH CONTROL AND ABORTION

Although living in a Catholic country, Victoria did not shy away from declaring her support of birth control and abortion. Indeed, she went even further and stated that it was a crime to bring a child into the world without wanting him.

> . . . I believe firmly that something that vitally concerns the woman, her body, has to depend principally on her, the protagonist. . . . Nobody asks a woman's opinion when it comes to war and military strategy. We are happy with things this way. War should be an obsolete activity, although it still is not. But in the business of giving life, *the opposite kind of activity,* women have to be the first people consulted.

> . . . I strongly believe that *life* is a sacrament. . . . But man does not hold life to be sacred when he goes to war. Why? If life is sacred, we would have to pass judgment on many of history's heroes who have been honored for not respecting life. If man pronounces the judgment that life is sacred when it has to do with deflecting the pollen or interrupting the development of an invisible masculine gamete that happens to have bumped into a female gamete, why does it stop being sacred when he sends thousands of strong, healthy boys, the best of our youth, to the slaughterhouse? I have never understood very well why, in the name of what masculine logic, war is not considered a crime but birth control and abortion are. (E-15:227–28)

Victoria wrote about a number of women, some just in passing, several at greater length, and an elect few as the subject of a major essay. The women to whom she gave honorable mention might figure in history, fiction, the creative arts, or the political scene; to each of them, for a brief moment, she gave life.

The following vignettes, taken directly from Victoria's words or in brief paraphrases, offer an idea of the range of the women who attracted Victoria and what she found interesting about them. While introducing these women to her readers, she also revealed a good deal of herself, putting into sharper focus her feelings about women.

Anna de Noailles—1933

In her essays, Victoria referred to Anna de Noailles as a great woman poet and a marvelous, irritating, and unique person. She claimed that she had two images of the French poet—one from her adolescence when she was transported by her lyricism, the other when she met the real person. She says that these two images registered on her mind without either of them completely negating the other, as happens when photographs are double-exposed. This vignette describes Victoria's first encounter with the French poet.

Not without emotion, I made my way one chilly evening in 1929 along la rue Scheffer where Anna lived. A mutual friend had told her that I was passing through Paris and she had written me, inviting me to come see her. I immediately accepted, although years before I had spiritually drawn away from her books and way of thinking. It was more like going to visit her on behalf of someone else who had once liked her very much.

La rue Scheffer fills with darkness as night falls, and in that darkness the doorman told me that she lived on the top floor. I entered the elevator, one of those asthmatic elevators that you find in certain Parisian buildings. The maid who opened the door led me through a salon literally jammed full of furniture and eighteenth-century art objects. It all reminded me of those salons that people never enter, to such a point that a vase of flowers there seems out of place. The tables, the chaise lounge, the chairs, the sofas seemed

133

grouped by chance, like hens in a farmyard. Moments later the maid returned to lead me into Mme. de Noailles, who, as was her custom, received visitors from her bed. I walked through the anteroom; the word "snug" spontaneously occurred to me to describe her bedroom, so pillowed and hermetic. It was crowded like the salon; Mme. de Noailles entertained herself in those days by painting, and her canvases were piled against the walls, on the chairs, the table, and the fireplace. Being careful not to knock anything over as I went by, I cautiously made my way to the narrow, high bed.

With her long, flowing black hair held back at the temples by yellow ribbons, her face is identical to her photographs. Immense dark eyes, aquiline nose . . . Nothing is imprecise in her features. Her shoulders, her long slender neck, her dark head . . . bobbing up at every moment, makes you think of some beautiful, cruel mix of swan and serpent. For there is in her something angelical and terrible. Something like fragility constructed of steel. Looking at her you see, above all, two things; her wild eyes and the movement of her hands, small, slender, and very pale. Looking at her eyes you say to yourself, "My God, how strong!" Looking at her hands: "My God, how fragile!"

But she has already started her loquacious, voluble chatter, and it is a new Anna de Noailles whom I am about to discover. She begins by reproaching me for my handwriting. She says that my writing bears absolutely no resemblance to my physical appearance and she wants to know which of the two is lying. My script is small, tiny, niggardly. I am large and I exude prodigality. She did not like my handwriting, but she liked me. I keep looking at her in suspense, and then I laugh.

After that she feels that she will be able to make me laugh as much as she wants; she senses how capable I am of savoring her remarks, the things that she comes out with. She laughs; she triumphs. She still is not blasé. She is flattered that I find her enchanting when she feels like being a little foolish.

She questions me about the difference between her height and mine. (She was minuscule.) She even has the urge to get out of bed to make exact comparisons. She assures me that both of us would figure very well in the population statistics in the Hachette almanac—I would represent Russia, she would stand for Belgium.

She asks me if I like her poetry and she answers the question herself: of course I like it since I am there. I tell her that, indeed, I have known it by heart ever since I was fifteen. She takes my hand, and as I press hers a little, she tells me that I have broken her bones. She embraces me then to thank me for my love of her verses and she continues talking nonstop. She tosses away one of her pillows, pulls it back, and then takes it again and puts it behind her head. She turns the light off and then on again. She interrupts herself to ask me if I am comfortable, if I am hot, if I am cold, if I am hungry, if I am thirsty, if my hat does not bother me. She wants me to take it off so she can look at my head. She wants me to stand up to prove that I am as big as I seemed to her when I entered the room. She asks me if I am happy: if the Spaniards seem like the Argentines; if I have sisters, if they are as tall as I am; if Keyserling is really a genius; if the Argentines become bored living in their country; what poets I like best; what philosophers; does Bergson interest me? Yes, he has written some wonderful pages. But he does not change the atmosphere of a room he enters. One must mistrust the genius of men who do not work this miracle. Einstein, yes, he certainly changes any room, a great genius. . . . Anna talks and talks, almost without giving you time to reply.

Afterward Victoria confessed that the spirit and loquacity of Mme. de Noailles had seduced her. "I asked myself in what moment of the day or night this dizzying woman might have found sufficient silence, sufficient darkness to turn to the truth in her heart and pull out of it some of those magnificent verses whose beauty is indisputable" (E-5:304–9).

Virginia Woolf—1934

These are Victoria's first impressions of Virginia Woolf, whom she originally met in London at an exhibition of Man Ray's photographs.

The evening before the opening some friends were going to get together in the room where the exhibition was to be held. Aldous Huxley invited me to go with him and he told me in confidence that perhaps Virginia would be there too.

Virginia went out very seldom and, according to what people told me, it was getting more and more difficult to meet her. You really couldn't count on her being there. So much so that, while I was looking at the people around me, I didn't try to guess if she was among them. Suddenly I heard her name and mine spoken by a friend. As I turned my head toward that voice, that marvelous face was already turned toward mine.

Imagine a mask, which even without life, without intelligence, would still be beautiful. Imagine that mask imbued with life and intelligence to such a point that it seemed to have been molded by them. Imagine all that, and still you will have poorly imagined the enchantment of the face of Virginia Woolf; enchantment of the most happy fusion of the material and the spiritual in a woman's face.

Virginia's face is beautiful not just because of its expression, but because of its architecture, because of its scaffolding. When we knew each other better, days later, I couldn't keep from saying to her, "It is the bones, Virginia, the bones that I find perfect"—a thing which made her laugh. Indeed, the beauty of this woman is of a deepness which is more than skin-deep, it is bone-deep.

The exaggeration of the eyebrows and the shape of her eyelids have a sleepy look. The mouth, with its full, tender lips, surprises because it seems to contradict the magnificent and rather cruel asceticism of her other features, particularly the nose, so fine, so spare. This mouth is admirably balanced, defended by a chin without weaknesses and without heaviness, a chin so fine that the delicate, offered sweetness of the lips becomes pathetic.

I was thinking all that, looking for the first time at the author of *Orlando,* in the midst of the comings and going of people in front of the photographs of Man Ray. Her forehead and her grey hair remained hidden beneath the wide brim of a hat which made her face paler and more delicate.

How old would she be? The same as Clarissa Dalloway, hardly past fifty. But I believe that she was never more attractive, although when she was younger it might have been in some other way. Everything that this woman has understood, and felt, now, at this moment, is emphasized in her face and comes together in her beauty. (E-22:77–79)

Ma Joad—1940

Victoria loved movies and often wrote film reviews for *Sur*—movies like *Wuthering Heights, The Bicycle Thief,* and *Lawrence of Arabia.* In 1940, in a review of *The Grapes of Wrath,* she spoke about the problem of translating a novel into a movie. Contrary to her usual experience, Victoria felt that the film interpretation of John Steinbeck's *The Grapes of Wrath* was "an almost perfect realization." She saw the movie as a social document that is "distressing and asphyxiating, but admirable." She realized that by flattering neither people nor things Hollywood did not rely on its usual film techniques to seduce the public. ("No fabulously long Greta Garbo eyelashes, no fabulously straight Robert Taylor teeth, no junky heroics, no cheap love affairs, or spectacular car chases.")

I believe that the only people who would like this movie are those who want to hear and say sane truths and those who defend democracy (at the same time that they believe it should purify itself). Because democracy is the only system that allows people who live surrounded by absurd lies to speak necessary, saving truths. What nation except a great democratic nation would permit the showing of a *mea culpa* like *The Grapes of Wrath?*

The time is the 1930s, in the middle of the tragedy of the dust bowl. Victoria introduces her reader to the Joads as they abandon their dried-up land and head for the golden promise of California in their run-down truck. She describes Tom, who has been in the penitentiary for killing a man in self-defense, and she tells about Preacher Jim Casey, who finds that "the sperit ain't in me no more." And then, after introducing the daughter, Rose of Sharon, and the hungry children, Victoria presents John Steinbeck's Ma Joad.

A person would have to be spiritually blind not to see anything more than poverty, ugliness, and hunger in *The Grapes of Wrath.* The mother in the Joad family, whom Jim Casey describes as "a woman so great with love she scares me," . . . is known to us only as Ma. . . . When Tom goes back to see Ma after four years in prison, his emotion does not register on his face. But Steinbeck communicates it to us in one of his most inspired pages when he describes her as her son sees her—with all the tenderness and knowledge of her that Tom bears in his soul and body.

Ma, with her housecoat faded from long wear and frequent washings, her ample body as resistant as those tree trunks that deeply understand the earth, her bare, broad feet, her strong arms, and her eyes that have looked so many sorrows squarely in the face, all are lacking in bodily perfection and are no longer at the age of physical charms. Nevertheless, Steinbeck, as he portrays Ma with a frying pan in one hand, speaks to us of something that is pure beauty. We see Ma's beauty the way we see a child's beauty (with purer eyes) or the beauty of those we love, who love us, because we perceive that beauty through the filter of our own tenderness and the tenderness we receive in return.

Ma knows that she cannot despair or falter without having her whole family waver and lose the vital energy they need to keep up the struggle. Slowly, over time, she has learned not to despair, not to falter, no matter what happens.

At the end of the novel, when Tom says good-bye to his mother, perhaps forever, he tells her that their separation should not afflict her as if it were definitive. "How'm I gonna know 'bout you?" the tormented Ma asks him. And Tom answers: "I'll be ever'where. Wherever you look. Whenever they's a fight so hungry people can eat, I'll be there. . . . I'll be in the way guys yell when they're mad an' I'll be in the way kids laugh when they're hungry an' they know supper's ready." Tom wants his mother to adopt all the sons she meets, that is, all of suffering humanity.

. . . Jim Casey could no longer preach, and Ma does not know how to speak, and Tom is a violent, desperate young man, but each of them, in his own way, by different paths, with different imperfections, come close to something that seems too much like true Christian love not to be so: love for one's fellow man.

All these things make their way to the screen with difficulty and with difficulty are expressed in cinematographic language. But those who bear these truths in their hearts cannot help but intuit them. Those who catch a glimpse of them are not mistaken. (E-23)

Nancy Astor—1964

Victoria was attracted to Nancy Astor, who she described as being as ardent a feminist as she was a Christian Scientist, a woman of great beauty and dynamism and the first woman to be admitted to the House of Commons, "that sacrosanct enclosure, reserved until then, for British men."

Nancy Astor's entrance into Parliament took place in 1919. It was more than a coronation. We all felt that if these doors were opening, others would not remain closed much longer. . . . In all the splendor of her maturity, of her beauty and her indomitable spirit, she avenged the suffragists by the sole act of existing. Let us be clear: she avenged them by not allowing society to ignore her existence as a responsible, conscientious human being. . . . The triumph of Lady Astor was the triumph of our cause. It was the end of a variety of sexual discrimination that is as strong as racial discrimination. . . . She disproved the myth of the unattractive, bitter, mannish feminist.

Victoria praised Nancy Astor for her useful work of bringing the concerns of women and children to the House of Commons. She wrote that Lady Astor always showed great courage, confronting difficult problems without fear or hesitation. In May of 1945 Lady Astor wrote Victoria that after twenty-five years in Parliament she was leaving, but leaving with regret because she felt that the times demanded a woman's voice in government. Victoria agreed that "never in the history of the world had there been a time when we so needed to have women in public affairs." She added, "I have never had political ambitions, but I want political careers to be accessible to women who choose to follow that path."

She then asked herself what important positions had been entrusted to women in the world and answered her own question by mentioning Golda Meir, the leader of Israel, and Sirimavo Bandaranaike, the first minister in Ceylon. Her next question was "Wouldn't it be a good idea to see what would happen if we gave greater participation to women in public affairs?" Her answer was a resounding "Yes"—something useful and good might result. It was not that she wanted to establish a matriarchal society. but rather that she wanted to see what would happen if women, following Nancy Astor's lead, were given a chance to take key roles in government (E-24).

Indira Gandhi—1966, 1968

Ever since reading Gandhi's biography in 1924, Victoria had a continuing interest in India. The time she later spent with Tagore, plus her relationship with Nehru, served to deepen the affinity. In 1960, Indira Gandhi, Nehru's daughter, arrived in Buenos Aires and there, in the Indian Embassy, awarded Victoria an honorary degree from Visva Bharati University.

> For a woman of the generations who struggled to win for half of humanity their rightful place (next to men), it is impossible not to consider the arrival of Indira Gandhi in our country as an unusual event of great importance. Not just because of her being prime minister, but also because, being a woman, she is in that office.

> Indira Gandhi says that ever since Mahatma Gandhi became the leader of the national movement in India, that country has grown accustomed to seeing women in the vanguard of political life. Women fought alongside their fathers, sons, husbands, brothers, and friends on a totally equal basis. All of them, insists the prime minister, rich and poor, educated and illiterate, those from the city and those from the countryside. This direct collaboration with men saved women from having to struggle against men (and against a good number of their own sex, as English and North American women had to do) before reaching their goals and achieving what the char-

ter of the United Nations today grants them (at least on paper). I single out women from England and North America because the suffragists of those two countries had a very special spirit of sacrifice and courage.

The tremendous thing about all this struggle in India was that it did more than save women from people who were indifferent to them. Remember the drama of the Brontës who concealed their talent as writers from their respected father. Remember Jane Austen who wrote in secret. And remember Virginia Woolf onto whom, according to indirect confession, her father projected an inferiority complex. And these are only three examples. Just think of Elizabeth Barrett who, thanks only to Browning, was able to leave the hated patriarchal prison and flourish as a writer and, even more important, as a human being. When a person struggles for justice with strangers, she can suffer a great deal. But when she struggles with people she loves it is a daily inferno.

Indira Gandhi was three times fortunate—a daughter of Nehru, a student of Tagore, and along with her father a friend of the Mahatma.[1] These three men believed in women. They believed that a woman was just as responsible as a man and as such they wanted her to assume positions of responsibility that would have a voice and a vote in everything that was done in India. They treated women as people who had a place on the same hierarchical ladder as men. Not as eternal minors. The Mahatma maintained this through his entire life. For those who have not known Tagore, or have not read him, it is sufficient to read his *The Home and the World* to understand his position about women. . . . As for Nehru, the following thoughts of his give an idea of the education his daughter received: "For my part, I have always been of the firm opinion that although it is possible to neglect a young man's education, it is not possible or desirable to neglect a young woman's education. The reasons are obvious. If women are educated it is probable that they will have an influence on men and will definitely influence their children. We talk about superior schools and colleges, no doubt important, but a person is shaped by the first ten years of his life. A great French writer once observed: 'If you want to speak about the condition of some country, tell me about the position of women in that country.'" (E-26:36–39)

Indira is an attractive woman in spite of not having inherited the very special good looks of her father. Her eyes are extraordinary—large and expressive. In Argentina we would call her long-nosed. But this nose that is perhaps too prominent for her face is what it is: one would not wish to have it altered by plastic surgery. I even believe that it gives more character to a face which is already so aristocratic. . . .

She speaks without hurrying, but without slowness, with a certainty that one would never call self-assurance, nor even serenity. It is, rather, the pleasing security of a person who knows just what she is saying and who never fears, nor has ever feared, to say it. In Indira there is a mixture of accepting softness and unshakable firmness. Absolute firmness. At least that was my impression.

Of what did we talk? Of the problems of women, naturally, and of how India was trying to solve them. Of the powerful support that the emancipation of women found in Gandhi and Nehru.

I felt that Indira had lived her entire life as a privileged person—privileged not by inherited riches, but by an adversity borne with dignity and patience. And privileged, too, by her association with a father who looked after her education with so much intelligence and real love. (E-25:193–94)

Isadora Duncan—1970

Victoria recalled that as a young girl living in Paris she had the wonderful experience of seeing Isadora Duncan dance. Victoria had responded enthusiastically to the rare beauty of the entire spectacle and especially to Duncan's spontaneous grace and perfection.

. . . That immense blue velvet curtain, the only decoration; her white Grecian tunic; her bare feet silently gliding over the stage, her face, illuminated from within and radiating with the pleasure of plunging into an invisible sea of delight, a sea where her body swam divinely.

Victoria realized that what made Isadora so special was the transformation of her material being into something spiritual. Learning from ancient Greek vases, Duncan gave the Greece of the Parthenon a contemporary interpretation and charged it with her own emotions.

. . . She restored the splendor of the movements of a distant era that had been set in marble and stone. She gave life to the statues because she knew how to instill them with human warmth; the warmth of her own body. She used no other material or mechanism. She wanted her body to freely express the pleasure, the happiness, the pain of being a living body.

For the young Victoria, Isadora Duncan had a talent and a genius that were inimitable. There would be other great dancers, she knew, but Isadora would remain untranslatable. That is why Victoria regretted seeing Vanessa Redgrave attempt to re-create the dancer on the screen. "Vanessa is not a dancer and it was a waste of her great talent to make her try to translate a language she did not know" (E-27).

Coco Chanel—*1971, 1977*

Victoria first met Coco Chanel in 1929, just before her disastrous rendezvous with Keyserling at Versailles. She had decidedly mixed feelings about the woman who had once been J.'s lover, but she was clearly fascinated by her and greatly admired her genius for designing simple, elegant clothes.

Victoria viewed Chanel as a strange, complex woman and was quite aware of her faults: her never disarmed arrogance, her tendency to cruel words, and her overly ambitious nature, always pressing for control and ready to do whatever was necessary to achieve her desire for money, fame, and power. All the same, Victoria gave Chanel full credit for her remarkable accomplishments in the fashion world, for her capacity for creation and work, and for her iron-tough will to succeed. Victoria considered that Chanel had single-handedly brought down the barricades in the fashion world by challenging male designers whom she perceived lacked sympathy with women and dressed them in outlandish costumes that both ridiculed and hobbled them. Victoria praised Chanel's unique talent, which imposed on fashion a change of direction that the times demanded. For Chanel saw that women in the 1920s needed unencumbering clothes, and she translated that need into stylish outfits. She introduced shorter skirts, more tailored, comfortable, go-anywhere clothes whose quality and design guaranteed that they would last for years.

Victoria herself wore Chanel's creations with great pleasure and proclaimed that Chanel's mastery for interpreting a woman's body in her own way, with grace and genius, was incomparable. Indeed, Chanel designed the gown that Victoria wore in Florence in 1939 for her triumphal role as narrator in Stravinsky's *Persephone*. Victoria's remarks about her fitting for this black lace gown are revealing:

> . . . The day of my last fitting, Mme. Therese wanted to have Chanel give the gown a good looking over. She went upstairs to get her and I, dressed and standing in front of the mirror that showed three flawless bodies, waited for her. Chanel did not come down. Mme. T., very disturbed, reported to

me that in view of the political tyranny in Italy at that time Chanel did not approve of my trip to Florence. Although not fully convincing, her reason seemed a respectable one. But later, when war with Germany broke out, when France was occupied by the Nazis and when, for me, the moment for absolute intransigence had come, I learned with surprise that Chanel did not seem to give the same importance to events that she did in May of 1939. Unforeseeable contradictions (E-28:124–25).

Victoria had heard the reports that, after Paris fell to the Germans, Chanel had slept with the enemy. Even so, Victoria, in writing about Chanel many years later, was able to see beyond her duplicity and veil of aloofness to the woman whose originality and designing magic had such a liberating and enduring influence on women's appearance and behavior (E-29).

Abigail Adams (1744–1818)—1975

Victoria introduced Abigail Adams to an Argentine audience, to which she was probably unknown, by noting that she was the wife of John Adams, the second president of the United States and the mother of John Quincy Adams, the sixth president.

. . . Abigail Adams reinforces my belief about the important influence of women, especially mothers, on men. In their first months and years of life, the child depends on her, materially and morally. According to scientists (my own opinion coincides with theirs but was born of pure intuition) the earliest childhood years leave indelible traces on people. From this understanding comes the necessity, as Jawaharlal Nehru advised, of giving women the same, or better, painstaking education as is given to men.

⊗

The union of John Adams and Abigail Smith must have been one of mutual influence. They lived together near Boston for the first ten years of their married life and they had one daughter and three sons. Then political responsibilities forced John to leave home while Abigail remained in charge of their children and the farm. Her education was quite minimal, the same, almost without exception, as all women in America (as well as other continents) received at that time. But she learned to write rather well, saying clearly what she wanted to say. She was passionately interested in independence, the cause that her husband was defending. However, as we will see, Abigail's opinions were not always John's. Probably they did not give the same importance to certain problems: concerns of women, for example. I have the impression that John gave way before the assaults of his wife.

꧁꧂

The separation of John and Abigail (for causes that were not voluntary, but were due to their patriotism) led to an extensive correspondence. They continued to be together in their thoughts. Many people think that absence makes couples grow apart, but I believe that a temporary physical separation is better than a habitual absence of a non-physical nature. . . .

꧁꧂

Their letters during this time of forced separation put in relief Abigail's intelligence and spirit. I ask myself what president's wife, past or present, anywhere in the world, would have written the letters that John Adams received. In this Year of the Woman [1975] little attention has been given to these letters from which I am going to quote. We are at the moment when the "Dear John," in the role of delegate to the First Continental Congress, leaves for Philadelphia in August of 1774; Abigail has to look after herself and, alone, tend to the education of her children. For a person of limited education, her successes are extraordinary.

Victoria then reproduces, in Spanish translation, excerpts from three of the letters from Abigail and John's correspondence. (They are transcribed here in their original English with their spelling and punctuation only slightly corrected.)[2]

Abigail Adams to John Adams, March 31, 1776

I have sometimes been ready to think that the passion for Liberty cannot be Eaquelly Strong in the Breasts of those who have been accustomed to deprive their fellow Creatures of theirs. Of this I am certain that it is not founded upon that generous and Christian principal of doing to others as we would that others should do unto us.

I long to hear that you have declared an independancy—and by the way, in the new Code of Laws which I suppose it will be necessary for you to make, I desire you would Remember the Ladies, and be more generous and favourable to them than your ancestors. Do not put such unlimited power into the hands of the Husbands. Remember all Men would be tyrants if they could. If perticuliar care and attention is not paid to the Ladies we are determined to foment a Rebellion, and will not hold ourselves bound by any Laws in which we have no voice, or Representation.

That your Sex are Naturally Tyrannical is a Truth so thoroughly established as to admit of no dispute, but such of you as wish to be happy willingly give up the harsh title of Master for the more tender and endearing one of Friend. Why then, not put it out of the power of the vicious and the Lawless to use us with cruelty and indignity, with impunity. Men of Sense in all Ages abhor those customs which treat us only as the vassals of your Sex.

John Adams to Abigail Adams, April 14, 1776

As to your extraordinary Code of Laws, I cannot but laugh. We have been told that our Struggle has loosened the bands of Government every where. That Children and Apprentices were disobedient—that schools and Colledges were grown turbulent—that Indians slighted their Guardians and Negroes grew insolent to their Masters. But your Letter was the first Intimation that another Tribe more numerous and powerfull than all the rest were grown discontented.

Depend upon it. We know better than to repeal our Masculine systems. Altho they are in full Force, you know they are little more than Theory. We dare not exert our Power in its full Latitude. We are obliged to go fair, and softly, and in Practice you know We are the subjects. We have only the Name of Masters.

Abigail Adams to John Adams, May 7, 1776

I can not say that I think you very generous to the Ladies, for whilst you are proclaiming peace and good will to Men, Emancipating all Nations, you insist upon retaining an absolute power over Wives. But you must remember that Arbitrary power is like most other things which are very hard, very liable to be broken—and, notwithstanding all your wise Laws and Maxims, we have it in our power not only to free ourselves but to subdue our Masters, and without violence throw both your natural and legal authority at our feet.

[Victoria comments] This correspondence between John and Abigail, written in a tone as from one equal to another, . . . is reassuring. John was not an idol for Abigail. Probably she *knew* him and she loved him. For John, Abigail was not a saint, a fairy, or some goddess from Olympus. He also knew her and loved her. Couples like this are what we want in this Year of the Woman, or in any other year. Abigail speaks as any one of us, young or old, would speak. She speaks as would those of us who believe that equality between men and women will bring about better understanding and greater mutual respect between them. Better children, perhaps. Better Love, with a capital L, without an atom of doubt. (E-30)

Susan Sontag—1975

"Any liberated woman who accepts her privileged position with complacency is an accomplice to the oppression of other women. I accuse a great majority of women of exactly this—women who have made careers in the arts and sciences, in the liberal professions and in politics."—SUSAN SONTAG

I met Susan Sontag this year, 1975, in Paris. She arrived at my hotel room followed by Edgardo Cozarinsky. I had read nothing of hers, though her name was familiar to me. She did not have even a remote idea of what I had written, but she knew about my struggle. . . . Today women know about one another this way.

Susan Sontag is the type of person who does not make too great an effort to win over people. Perhaps it was because of this quality that she immediately conquered me. Right away I saw her physical beauty, untouched by any makeup (an allegorical figure for a new Michelangelo, I thought). And then I became aware that seated before me was someone whose intelligence had the brilliance of precious stones that have been carefully cut and polished.

. . . Susan Sontag enjoys undoubted advantages compared with me: when she was a student the times were considerably more favorable for developing talents than were my times. I estimate that Susan would be somewhere in the neighborhood of forty. That means that she was twenty around 1955, while I turned twenty in 1910. Between two women of the twentieth century, forty-five years makes for enormous differences in possibilities, circumstances, experiences, education, and freedom. An exquisite stone, skillfully cut, and an unfinished stone.

However, as we were talking, I could see that there is nothing in Susan's reactions to women's liberation that was not for years also part of my own thinking. Only that the reparations to women that fill the newspapers and magazines these days seemed in my day to be due to the craziness of just a few women. In 1975 (the Year, it seems, of the Woman) such retributions are

guaranteed and have become the right of citizens in the privileged places
of this Earth. In our country, although they continually sing the praises of
the mother, they still do not give her legal control of her own life. They treat
us women like a herd of more or less sacred cows.

The arrival of Susan Sontag at the Trémoille Hotel one sad winter afternoon was for me an appearance that changed the gray of the weather
and my worries. She could not know how interesting that was for me, not
realizing what it was to turn twenty in 1910. I, conscious of the past and
of the present, was enchanted by such an intrepid, well-honed, flexible intelligence. Enchanted the way a mother who has not seen her young daughter for a long time unexpectedly meets her as an adult, giving life to her
dream (a dream that the mother did not realize, although she knew that in
attempting to fulfill it she had gone to great lengths and challenged mythological monsters).

This unknown person whose presence incited me to leaf through the
inventory of my past was not simply a possible new friend; she was the silent
daughter, immediately recognized as such, and suggesting something well
beyond friendship.

The following day when I went looking for her books, the bookstore only
had one volume of essays left. The essays were of the same level that I had
discerned the afternoon before, although they did not reveal her literary side.
To my great surprise when I returned from Europe I found, in my bedroom
in San Isidro, a few pages taken from *Temps Modernes* giving Susan's answers
to a 1972 interview on the status of women. They seemed to be waiting
for me and they clarified the reason for my sudden sense of *recognition.* Susan
Sontag was living what I had thought before she was born, and on top of that
she had been educated to communicate her thoughts better than I had.
All this and talent too. Hallelujah!

My letters as an adolescent and as a young woman, saved by a friend, document the similarity of what we each were writing. My letters are without
value except that there is in them a stammering effort to say what Susan Sontag was going to articulate in such an impressive way. Children of the flesh
are often more unfaithful to our aspirations than those apparently born of
our dreams.

⌘

Susan Sontag, with reason, points to certain virtues that are considered
essentially male: courage, loyalty, rationality, rectitude. However, women are

continually giving the lie to that prejudice. When there is explosive, undeniable proof that a woman possesses these virtues, she is called exceptional.
Who has not heard such praise as "She has a man's mind"? And who hasn't
observed that the praise is not rejected. But it is denigrating. As many
women as men can be exceptional because of their talents (whatever those
talents may be). When women are exceptional it is not because they seem
like the sex that has a monopoly on intellectual excellence; they are talented in their own right. Despite belonging to another, much later, generation, Susan Sontag had stumbled upon the same old genial masculine invention: the talented woman who has talent only in the measure that she
seems like a man.

Susan Sontag does not tolerate women who, being exceptional, do not
feel a sense of solidarity with their sisters and puff themselves up as they
enter, alone (always with a title indicating something rare), the exclusive circle of chosen men. I have known some extreme cases. The Countess de
Noailles, for example. . . . She believed in the absolute superiority of men. . . .
Susan Sontag, just as I do, repudiated this attitude. . . . When Susan enters the enemy camp she wants to enter with her whole army. She is im-
pervious to masculine adulation.

        ෫

. . . Susan thinks, as do I, that the privileges given men form part of the very
basis of society and that men will not renounce these privileges for simple
reasons of humanity and justice. This is the crux of the problem. We are, and
we will continue to be, second-class citizens until this unfortunate wrong
is overcome. And it is a mistake to think that it affects only women. It harms
the couple.

The so accepted, and honored, feminine virtue of influencing her companion by enchanting him, by praising him, by flattering him, is one of
the arts that we will have to undermine and ridicule. But there are still men,
especially, I suppose, Latin ones, who are addicted to this kind of servile behavior.

Susan believes that the liberation of women is a necessary *first step* toward
the construction of a just society and not the reverse, as Marxists main-
tain. . . . She advises women to make concrete demands on themselves:
not to be so preoccupied with their physical appearances (for example, not
to submit to the tyranny of fashion), not to set foot in a beauty shop, etc.
I dare to tell her that it makes no difference to her because she is beautiful

without any effort, without the help of Elizabeth Arden or Revlon. I don't know how much I agree with these restrictions that apply to our beautification, clothes, and makeup. Certainly no one has to accept the stupid mandates of fashion, with their orders and counter-orders, and the command to put on makeup as if it were armor to seduce the innocent: the boss, the no-account tyrant at home. . . .

I do not agree with all of Susan's points of view. I do not accept the idea of sometimes resorting to violence, but I see very well what brought her to think in those terms. I hope that she reflects on this. I respect her. With pleasure I yield to her. (E-31)

Emily Brontë

Victoria's reading of *Wuthering Heights* and Mrs. Gaskell's biography of Charlotte Brontë helped her to understand the torments that shaped Emily Brontë's everyday life and literary world. This essay is an abridged version of a lecture that Victoria Ocampo gave on June 14, 1938, to a meeting sponsored by *Sur* and held at the Women's League Library in Buenos Aires. It later served as the introduction to the first Argentine edition of *Wuthering Heights*.

If ever there was a person who might have been confused with the place where she was born and with the things that surrounded her, it was Emily Brontë. For the wind blowing at this moment in Yorkshire is the wind breathed in *Wuthering Heights*. This book is a place, an image of the title it bears. But this place, identifiable on maps of England, is more than England: it is the soul of Emily Brontë. The soul of Emily is here in the Americas, as it is in any part of the world, just as much as in England. Emily Brontë's soul goes beyond the map of her country and, as it does, brings us close to her. For this reason, *Wuthering Heights* is ours. Because of this, Yorkshire, where we have never been, miraculously becomes ours too. Thus, obliquely, poets help us to encounter our own country in theirs and even those most rooted in their own land are united with all lands. I have never understood better what the great harsh wind of the pampas, with its screeching tero birds, meant to me than when I listened to the moan of the wind of *Wuthering Heights*. That wind can only be heard by those who are already familiar with a similar lament: the complaining wind that arises from their own native land, from their own inalienable wilderness.

The Brontë sisters have been written about extensively. But while Charlotte has left numerous documents for her biographers, Emily withdraws from the eager eyes of her admirers. Besides her novel, her poems, things Charlotte wrote about her, and some stories that Charlotte's friends told, there is nothing that lets us follow her trail. Emily was, during her lifetime, a person of wild reserve. She continues to be inaccessible after death. Emily had no celebrity while she lived and this permitted her to remain in the shadows; shadows that continue to protect her from curious eyes. The most direct way to encounter her (other than in her writings) is to inventory the things surrounding her.

The family into which a woman is born and in which she grows up has profound influence on her, even when she differs from that family, even when she contradicts it, even when she becomes estranged from it, even when she reacts against it. In the case of the Brontë family, because of its sense of unity and the isolation to which it was condemned by its remoteness, the family came to exercise a kind of spell. Paralyzed by this—let us not forget what the family signified in the Victorian age—Charlotte and Emily lived their lives by holding their genius in check, the way one holds one's breath around someone who is gravely ill.

Emily's father, the Reverend Patrick Brontë, began by not noticing this genius, expecting the advent of glory by way of Branwell, his only son. In a family made up of five girls and one boy, could it come through any other door? After his wife's death, Reverend Brontë became solitary. He ate alone and he would go out for long walks on the moors. His contacts with the world were limited to those required by his parish ministry. His ideas on bringing up children were Spartan. Patrick Brontë wanted his children to become indifferent to the pleasures of eating and dressing well, of comfort and luxury, and he was almost sadistic in his single-minded dedication to this goal.

But to raise five girls and a boy it was absolutely necessary for the Reverend Brontë to have a feminine presence at his side. He turned to Miss Branwell, one of his wife's sisters, who was well on her way to becoming an old maid. . . . She was an English woman of upright character, scrupulous, but narrow-minded—as was the style of the times—and incapable of understanding the special genius of that strange nest of little chicks. Miss Branwell gave her nieces sewing lessons and taught them the art of managing a house.

The Reverend Brontë intervened in his children's education in a quite original way. He talked to them as if they were adults, he conversed with them, even about politics, he made them read aloud, he told them hair-raising stories. When the oldest of his children was ten and the youngest four, suspecting that his offspring understood more than it appeared, he devised a scheme to promote their self-confidence. Calling his children to him he put a mask on each of them in turn, imagining that by protecting them with that disguise they would feel more comfortable answering his questions. When he interrogated Branwell, the only boy in the family, he posed the following problem: "What is the best way of knowing the difference between the intellects of men and women?" "By considering the difference between their bodies," the boy answered. Given that Branwell was less than ten years old, the Reverend Brontë's question is rather surprising. Undoubtedly father and son soon decided to proclaim the superiority of the male intellect. Charlotte and Emily always felt somewhat guilty, a little inhibited by being women and by writing with more success than the men in the family. The proof of this is that the sisters hid the publication of their book from Branwell for fear of humiliating him. Charlotte assures us that her brother never knew that his sisters had published a line. As for the Reverend Brontë, it was kept from him as long as possible.

A second circumstance had grave consequences for the Brontë girls: Cowan Bridge. This was a boarding school run by the Reverend Carus Wilson for the education of daughters of indigent parsons. Built in a swampy area, the school seems to have been especially pernicious at that time. The food was abominable and the care given the girls was enough to ruin the health of even the most robust. Reverend Brontë undoubtedly had no clear idea of the prison to which he had sentenced his daughters. Charlotte and Emily survived Cowan Bridge, but neither of them would ever forget that cruel experience, which must have left scars on their bodies and hearts. All their lives they were obsessed by the memory of the suffering and death of their sisters, Maria and Elizabeth, fed food "unfit for pigs," dying of the cold in the foreboding dampness of the dormitories and given sermons on the eternal fire and the need to struggle against gluttony, all as a way to assuage their cold and hunger.

When the surviving Brontë girls returned home from Cowan Bridge, luck at last brought happiness and warmth to their lives. A new servant, Tabby, arrived at the parsonage. She would live with the Brontës for thirty years. Tabby was one of those admirable village women, unschooled and full of good sense, skilled and zealous in her duties, hardworking, quick to obey, but also quick to give orders. She immediately became a member of the family. When, years later, she broke her leg and the Reverend Brontë and Miss Branwell talked of replacing her, the three sisters, generally so respectful of their father's wishes, were adamantly opposed. Emily declared that Tabby was not to leave the house under any condition and that she, Emily, would take over her work. She kept her word. To carry out Tabby's duties meant to sew, iron, sweep, and bake bread.

Tabby knew how to make her kingdom, the kitchen, a refuge for the four children. There she taught them to peel potatoes and would discuss with them whether or not to light a candle as night was falling—it was necessary to economize. There, watching over her casseroles, she told them endless stories about fairies, ghosts, the superstitions of the Yorkshire people, and the tragedies of local families. I visualize a breathless Emily drinking in these stories. And when she wrote *Wuthering Heights,* it is a servant woman who is charged with telling us the tragedy of Catherine Earnshaw and Heathcliff. In that solitude and silence of the village, in that nearness to the deserted moor, each small event, each face, each object, each story told around the fire, was to have endless echoes in Emily's imagination. Everything must have been magnified, everything must have touched on the supernatural.

Deprived of a mother, living with a father who tended to solitude and was preoccupied with stoicism, under the thumb of a well-intentioned but cold aunt who had little imagination, the Brontë children turned to each other for solace. They adored each other and lived for one another.

Their chief entertainment was of a literary, imaginative order, and as often happens in large families, the two oldest of the surviving children (Charlotte and Branwell), and the two youngest (Emily and Anne), formed inseparable pairs. Each of them chose favorite heroes, they invented characters and histories, and took possession of entire islands. Thus Charlotte was Wellington while Emily decided to appropriate Aran Island. The selection of this island seems mysteriously in keeping with Emily's deserted, savage destiny. Charlotte and Branwell, Emily and Anne moved from childhood to adolescence, from adolescence to youth, without ever abandoning a world created by fantasy, a world filled with imaginary characters. The kingdom of Angria, invented by the older children, led them to use oceans of ink. The younger ones played a game similar to living in a dream world and invented the country of Gondal which they must have inhabited more than the parsonage. When Emily, at nine, chose for her kingdom an island that is made of pure majestic rock whipped by waves and winds, she is already rehearsing the scene, the drama for which she was born. To come in touch with herself, Emily needed to make contact with things, and everything around her was arid and deserted, like Aran Island, devoid of arable land.

The moors were the only place the Brontës had on which they could run, walk, or wander freely. These moors of Yorkshire, like our Pampas, are a monotonous landscape, tedious and repetitious, picturesquely poor for those who don't know them intimately and so don't carry them in their inner being. The imagination capable of finding pleasure in them can't be, as Charlotte tells us, the "gentle dove" type, but rather a kind of "solitude-loving raven." Emily nourished herself with this landscape and identified with it to such an extent that she was not able to live without the moor. Three times she abandoned it to go to school, or to earn her living, and three times she became sick, longing for her home. The heather on the moor, the great silent spaces where only the wind speaks, increasingly became the necessary accompaniment for all her thoughts, for all her emotions, for all her poetic creation.

In the parsonage Emily read, wrote, ironed, and cooked. For relaxation she would run on the moor with her dog Keeper. Mrs. Gaskell (who is our most reliable source of information) asserts that Emily made the bread for the household and that her literary preoccupation never prevented the bread from being light and tasty.[1] She also mentions that anyone passing the kitchen door might see Emily with a book propped up in front of her, perhaps studying German as she kneaded dough. It was common to see books in the kitchen, she says. We know what books were in Emily's hands at sixteen: Milton, Shakespeare, Goldsmith, Pope, Byron, Campbell, Wordsworth, Southey, Johnson, Hume, Boswell.

At nine in the evening, with the work of the day behind them, once the Reverend Brontë and Miss Branwell had retired, the girls at last had a chance to talk to their hearts' content. It was useless for the Reverend Brontë to shout at them, as he invariably did as he wound the old clock: "Don't be late to bed." In all times, in all countries, fathers have issued this order and children have disobeyed: the night lingered on in unending conversations.

During Christmas vacation in 1836 Charlotte wrote to Southey, sending him a sample of her poetry. Southey replied and in the most lamentable way. The letter began like this: "You evidently possess, and in no inconsiderable degree, what Wordsworth calls the 'faculty of verse.' I am not depreciating it when I say that in these times it is not rare."[2] Original statement! The poetic gift in Southey's time, as in all times, was extremely rare. The literary history of countries richest in poetic endeavors proves that to us. Then Southey goes from foolishness to the Victorian commonplace par excellence: "Literature cannot be the business of a woman's life, and it ought not to be. The more she is engaged in her proper duties, the less leisure will she have for it, even as an accomplishment and a recreation."[3] Poor Southey, so sure of himself and his unshakeable principles! This letter, this extremely misguided statement, not worthy of his talent, was addressed to the parsonage at Haworth where a girl of genius, the indefatigable Emily, was willingly carrying out the duties of household maid and, in her free moments, was preparing one of the most extraordinary novels of the nineteenth century.

The blow leveled by Southey at the Brontës in the person of Charlotte does not dishearten the girls. When one reads and, even more, when one writes for the same reason that one drinks and eats, such an infliction may injure but it does not kill. Charlotte, after digesting Southey's letter—which didn't seem as bad to her as it now appears to us—wrote to Wordsworth. But experience had taught her a lesson. This time she signed with initials, giving no indication of her sex. Impossible to combat sexual prejudice in any other way, at least for the moment, Charlotte thinks. Wordsworth is perplexed by the letter. He doesn't know whether to attribute it to some clerk in a law office or to a dressmaker intoxicated by literature. Neither the illustrious Southey nor the illustrious Wordsworth had good intuition.

In the autumn of 1845, Charlotte chanced upon the manuscript of Emily's poems. This discovery caused Emily great chagrin; the idea that other eyes than hers might read her poems seems to have been absolutely intolerable. This makes us think that she considered the poems to be violently autobiographical and that she imagined with horror that by reading them Charlotte might have the key to some interior drama; the key, at least, to a sensibility zealously guarded.

Emily did not think of herself as a great poet. She did not recognize that the privilege that was bestowed on her genius was the power to speak of human beings in general by speaking of herself and that, in more than one sense, the "I am the other" of Rimbaud was true for her, as for all great poets. Emily did not realize that the readers to whom her poetry was directed would never have the impression as they read her that they were indiscreetly peeking into her life, but instead would be motivated to take a sounding of their own lives.

Charlotte succeeded in calming her sister's indignation. Anne, encouraged by Emily's example, confessed that she too had written verses. Charlotte finally decided that the poems of all three deserved to be published. Neither Southey nor Wordsworth had weakened her faith. But how to carry it off? " . . . we did not like to declare ourselves women, because—without at the time suspecting that our mode of writing and thinking was not what is called 'feminine,' we had a vague impression that authoresses are liable to be looked on with prejudice; we noticed how critics sometimes use for their chastisement the weapon of personality, and for their reward, a flattery, which is not true praise."[4]

Here Charlotte touches on something that all women who write know from experience, even in our day. But the repulsive mixture of condescension and praise still offered to women writers was much more nauseating in the Victorian era. It must have had an emetic effect on the delicate stomachs of its victims. What to invent so as not to have to swallow that emetic? Mary Ann Evans invents a name, calling herself George. George Eliot; but above all, George. George is what is important to men. The Brontë sisters call themselves Currer (Charlotte), Ellis (Emily), and Anton (Anne) Bell. As they did in their childhood, they will put on masks. But this time the masks will be of their own choosing and, thus protected, they will speak.

Emily's poems come as a cry and make us ask ourselves why they were not immediately heard. Charlotte later acknowledged that they were the only poems of real merit in the book. When Virginia Woolf sums up her opinion of Emily's work she writes with the admirable precision of her intelligence: "Hers, then, is the rarest of all powers. She could free life from its dependence on facts; with a few touches indicate the spirit of a face so that it needs no body; by speaking of the moor make the wind blow and the thunder roar."[5] And she believes that Emily, a poet above all, has used her rare powers in these poems and that she will live on even more through them than through *Wuthering Heights*.

In these poems, Emily's austerity, her passion, her nakedness, her blending of hell and heaven reveal something of what Heathcliff and Catherine are going to say to us:

Oh! could I see thy lids weighed down in cheerless woe;
Too full to hide their tears; too stern to overflow;
Oh! Could I know thy soul with equal grief was torn,
This fate might be endured, this anguish might be borne.
How gloomy grows the night! Tis Gondal's wind that blows;[6]

And the wind of Gondal is the wind of the novel. It blows in the poems and in Emily's novel. This accompaniment calms her, perhaps because there is in her very depths, "A wilder sound than mountain wind."

Like the moor with only the heather in its purple splendor, like Emily herself whose unforgettable eyes don't appear to have ever taken pleasure in a mirror which would let her recognize her luminous beauty, the strange poems of this strange girl are devoid of adornment or of any preoccupation with adornment. Emily listened to her own self, but she never saw herself. If the magnificent cascade of her hair or her verses have ever impressed her, it has been while untangling them; she has felt their weight as she untied them, but she never braided them into a crown.

Between Emily and her God there are no intermediaries, between Emily and her predilection for the Infinite, for the Absolute, there are no books, no sermons. Communications are direct. Emily cannot accept the manufactured confection, the "ready-made" aspect of religions:

Vain are the thousand creeds
that move men's hearts.[7]

But it is precisely because of the image of God that she bears within herself ("O God within my breast"), because of her thirst for God, that God is in her. The God of Emily is too great for ceremonies, too great for the petty, cruel, demeaning interpretations that man sometimes has of God. If she had been better known, Emily could have been taken for a heretic just as her book was seen as pagan. Emily was a heretic as are many of those few people for whom religious feeling is not simply skin-deep, but rather is something profound, which touches the most vital roots of the human being. Sometimes such heretics are saints.

As for her passionate love poems, it is important to know to whom they were directed. Sometimes the beings who most fascinate us are fantasies given life by our own life. Emily was enchanted by a phantom; what we don't know is if this phantom was the phantom of a man or the phantom of a phantom. It's all the same. Was it called William Weightman, the young, attractive minister who came to assist the Reverend Brontë and who died while Emily was in Brussels? Was it called Louis Parensell? Nothing proves it was, nothing proves it wasn't, and, I repeat, it's all the same. The love poems are there, undeniable in their beauty, as undeniable as the terrible passion which ends in destruction in *Wuthering Heights.*

Wuthering Heights was published in December of 1847, exactly one year before the death of its author, and it was very badly received by the critics. Emily was destined never to know the place that this book would have in English literature.

While the Brontës lived, *Wuthering Heights* was attributed to Charlotte, who protested vigorously. After her death the novel was declared to have been written by Branwell, which is even more absurd. People considered that the book's style was too fiercely masculine to belong to a woman. The harshly manifested passions, the unbridled hatred, the obstinate friendships, the uncouth savagery of the Yorkshire people, can be shocking to readers who have never lived in that region, Charlotte timidly concedes. For she herself is a lit-

tle intimidated by *Wuthering Heights,* as she was by Emily. Charlotte rec-
ognizes that there hangs over the novel a horror of great darkness; that in
it we breathe the electricity of storms. She is sure about the terrible beauty
of this book, but she almost wants to ask pardon for Heathcliff, the hero who
bears Hell within himself. If Emily has created him, if she has created
Catherine Earnshaw, it is because she could do nothing less. The artist works
passively under the dictates of a force that she cannot control, nor sup-
press, nor change, Charlotte tells us.

In the dough of *Wuthering Heights* that her quick hands knead as new
bread, Emily mysteriously blends the known and the unknown; what she
has seen and what she imagines, what she has felt and what she has a hunch
might happen; what she knows and what she guesses, what she possesses and
what will never be bestowed upon her. All this belongs to her in equal measure, it is cast at the same temperature, it shares one environment, the environment of Emily Brontë.

The novel unfolds on that moor that she knows, on which she lives, where
she has grown like the heather, where the wind has howled in unison with
her heart. That moor is not a landscape that she feels compelled to describe,
but rather an extension of her very self which it is imperative to express.
Because written expression is a compelling necessity for great quiet people
like Emily Brontë.

How has Emily prepared herself to describe characters so marked and diverse? What models did she have? Her practical knowledge of the inhabi-
tants of Haworth, with its simple country people or squires, is almost nil.
Charlotte says that this knowledge is comparable to what a nun could ac-
quire by watching the local people pass by the bars of her convent window. Nevertheless, Charlotte attests, Emily had captured their ways, their
language, she was in touch with their lives, with their family histories, even
down to the smallest details.

I believe there can be no doubt of the similarity of temperament that
binds Emily Brontë to her protagonist. When Heathcliff says to Nelly, "My
spirit is so eternally confined," it is Emily who is telling us how and why she
has written *Wuthering Heights.* Emily was a passionate, violent, tumultuous,
wild being—like her two protagonists. But she only dared to live in ac-
cord with her temperament through Catherine and Heathcliff. Her passion,
her violence, her tumult burst out in them and broke their dikes with such
awful force that there was no escape.

Emily is Catherine, Emily is Heathcliff. When she walks on the moor, in
the midst of a silence where the cries she doesn't cry resound in a thou-

sand echoes, when there in that solitude, her inner tumult, her comings and goings between hell and heaven, become more evident to her, Catherine and Heathcliff break loose from her and live through her.

I see Emily Brontë in the prison of the Haworth parsonage walking round and round the dining room table, like a young animal; I see her in an epoch that was, for her, another prison: the Victorian prison; I see her on the moor, that immense prison where she could at least breathe and run: I see her, finally, in that infinite jail that is the solitude of a spirit eternally turned inward upon itself. (E-32)

Victorian Fathers

This essay is a chapter in Victoria Ocampo's book *Virginia Woolf en su diario.*

Reading Sophocles, Virginia Woolf compares Electra with Emily Brontë. She sees the same kind of feminine heroism in Greece as in England. But Electra suffered under a more oppressive burden and more suffocating customs than those which the Victorian taboos imposed. Nevertheless, some Greek prohibitions were the exact equivalent of the one Virginia sums up by the phrase "a maid and a hansom cab."[8] The daughter of a prominent man had to be married before she could walk alone through Piccadilly and before she could go out by herself in a cab. She wouldn't have dreamed she could do so daring a thing without stirring up her whole family. Like most of my contemporaries, I have gone through this experience. It always seemed grotesque to me.

The maid, Virginia observes in *Three Guineas,* had an important role in the life of the English upper classes (and the same was true in Argentina) until the onset of the war in 1914. The maid escorted not only young girls, but also married women. I have known some women who felt secretly flattered because their husbands would not permit them to go out in a taxi without taking a maid along as a chaperone. An interesting book could be written on the theme: "The role of the maid in the leisure classes." Some maids became very important in the life of their mistresses—take, for example, Elizabeth Barrett's maid. But that is another story. I am referring here to the services that the fathers or husbands entrusted to the maids and not to those that the maids rendered according to their own judgment and character. Virginia sarcastically emphasizes that after a certain time the protection of chastity by maids becomes too costly an item for the bourgeois budget.

In order for a young girl to "preserve her body intact for her future husband" (*whatever that may mean*), who generally didn't restrain from wild escapades; in order for a wife to avoid the risk of being unfaithful to a husband who rarely devoted his fidelity to her, nothing better was found than to put those females (this is the name that squares with such treatment) under the custody of another female in whom, one doesn't know by what characteristic aberration of masculine logic, one had more confidence.[9]

Virginia Woolf felt passionately about this matter, and thanks to this she was able to give her writing full measure of her satirical spirit, of her sense of the comical, just as she revealed her love for fairness and her blessed indignation in the face of all dictatorial attitudes. *A Room of One's Own* and *Three Guineas* are the true history of the Victorian struggle between the victims of the patriarchal system and the patriarchs, between the daughters and the fathers and brothers. Virginia ended up by telling these despots: Consider, reason, reflect for a moment. Our struggle, the one of women against the tyranny of the patriarchal conditions imposed by you, is analogous to the struggle that you were later to engage in against the tyranny of the fascist, Hitlerist state.

Our struggle was not merely about "*a maid and a hansom cab,*" nor the prohibition of smoking cigarettes (things that became important, disquieting, as symptoms, because of the prohibition itself). Our struggle also concerned the right to choose a husband and a career. The case of the Reverend Patrick Brontë was not an isolated case, nor did it in any way provoke the censure of the society of its time. This Anglican minister became famous only because Charlotte Brontë, the victim, was famous. It was a common case. When the author of *Jane Eyre* wanted to marry Nicholles (another minister, a respectable man in the sense in which the elder Brontë understood respectability, consequently making Nicholles acceptable as a son-in-law), her father forbade the marriage. There was no motive other than caprice, beyond the desire to keep Charlotte for himself, for his exclusive service. For months the poor girl submitted, suffered, debated with herself. She didn't dare rebel for fear that her father's health might be jeopardized, for fear that an act of unusual insubordination might be a mortal blow to him. (Oh, such innocence. The Reverend finally died of old age. She was the one who was to die in the full bloom of youth when the stubborn patriarch finally consented to her marriage, which lasted less than a year.) Society of the Victorian era remained undaunted by the conduct of the Reverend Brontë. However, as Virginia notes, if he had publicly tortured a dog, or stolen a watch, his reputation would have suffered. But in this sense a girl had less worth than a dog or a watch, and her father was able to give free rein to what today in the United States is cause for divorce: mental cruelty.

The truth of this assertion is found in the post-Victorian English newspapers of June 5, 1913, and the following days, where there are comments on "a tragic page in the history of the Derby." Anmer, one of the king's horses, was "ignominiously intercepted in his race by a female." The death of Miss Davison, the suffragette who threw herself under the feet of the animal, is not regarded as a tragic occurrence (the condolences go to the "turf"), but as a grotesque and shameful act. *The Pall Mall Gazette* says: "There can only be pity for the dementia which led an unfortunate woman to seek a grotesque and meaningless kind of 'martyrdom' in the fancied interests of a political cause. . . . The interests of Women's Suffrage have not been promoted by the stopping of the King's horse. . . . The public will rather be confirmed in the view that political excitement has a disastrous effect upon certain types of feminine nature, and deepened in its misgivings as to the amount of wisdom which a new electorate that can produce such advocates can bring to the service of the State. The tragedy, or semi-tragedy, of Tattenham Corner was inspired by emotions that have more kinship with the grossest pagan superstitions than with the progressive intelligence of English womanhood."[10]

Emily Wilding Davison's death became a rallying cry for the women's movement in England. The following afternoon the Women's Social and Political Union (WSPU) met to pay tribute to her. Emmeline Pankhurst, the militant suffragette who founded the WSPU in 1903, could not herself be present as she was in hiding from the police. Instead, a letter from her was read to the assembled women proclaiming that one of their bravest soldiers had left them. Mrs. Pankhurst declared that Miss Davison had gladly laid down her life for women's freedom and that the world was filled with awe and admiration by her heroism.

At the inquest on June 10, Joscelyne Davison identified the body of his half-sister. He said that she was thirty-eight years old, had lived in Long Horsley, Northumberland, and had been passionately devoted to the cause of enfranchisement for women. He testified that there was nothing to lead him to suppose that his sister was mentally abnormal, that she had a B.A. from London University, and had passed with honors at Cambridge. He described her as a person of considerable gifts, both as a speaker and as a prolific writer.

On June 14 the body of Emily Davison was taken by train to London. At Victoria Station the funeral procession was joined by about three thousand women, all in black, white, or purple dresses and carrying Madonna lilies and other flowers. The cortege was divided into eleven sections, each with its own band and banner bearer, and in the middle of the procession was the coffin, in an open hearse covered with flowers.

Very slowly, through immense crowds, they walked toward St. George's Church in Bloomsbury for the memorial service. Behind the hearse the brougham which was to have carried Mrs. Pankhurst remained empty. She had been arrested as she was leaving her apartment to go to the funeral and was sentenced to three years imprisonment. Behind the empty brougham marched groups of hunger strikers, women doctors, women in academic gowns, and about a dozen surpliced clergy.[11]

Evidently the life of Anmer was valued infinitely more than that of Miss Davison in those times (hardly forty-one years ago). I have looked over extensive information on that event in an enormous book of clippings about Craganour ("the disqualified winner of the Derby"), which is religiously preserved at the Chapadmalal estate. The splendid animal sleeps solemnly under a stone that bears his name in the beautiful park on the estate. I don't know if Miss Davison, in some place in England, will have such a poetic tomb. I offer to writers this theme for meditation and this title: "Ballad of the Tomb of Craganour, disqualified victor of the Derby, whose glorious name filled the English newspapers in June of 1913, while that of the obscure Miss Davison, killed as just punishment for her 'bad behaviour,' hardly appeared on the third page. R.I.P."

The Victorian and post-Victorian fathers who acted in ways similar to Patrick Brontë today form a great multitude of anonymous and forgotten shadows. If their hardness of heart and their infantile egotism (in which psychiatrists today would detect some fixation) has been forgiven in heaven, so much the better. Here on earth Virginia Woolf has settled accounts with them in *Three Guineas,* without ever abandoning her enchanting and implacable smile.

She never underestimated, as other ungrateful and ignorant women have, what the woman of today owes to her heroic sisters of the past, the suffragettes, the feminists, who were treated with contempt, reviled, ridiculed. Their battle, our battle, was long and fierce.

This is what happened to us in Argentina around 1935: a reform of the Civil Code threatened the limited rights which had already been won by women. With respect to the economic aspects of life, married women were to share the fate of minors and the insane. Without authorization from her husband, according to the projected reform, a woman would not be able: first, to work in any profession, industry, or business; second, to freely dispose of the product of her labor; third, to administer her property (the husband was to be its responsible, legal administrator); fourth, to become a member of any society, civil, commercial, or etc.; fifth, to make or receive donations.

The matter appeared to us so senseless and serious that some friends and I decided to protest to the magistrates who were to decide on the reform. It fell to me to visit two of these magistrates, one of them an important person. This last man felt it was reasonable and healthy, for example, for a woman to need the consent of her husband, not only to work outside her home—of course, in her house she could break her back from sunrise to sunset—but also to carry on a professional career. It is necessary, the magistrate said, that there be a head of the family, just as there is a captain on a ship. Otherwise, there would be confusion in the home. What would happen if a woman got it into her head to work in an office as a typist? She would leave her children in the hands of hired help, she would neglect the household chores, she would abandon her husband since there wouldn't be time for watching over his material well-being. I answered him that the ladies who spend their lives in dress shops, in movies, in theaters, at cocktail parties, at bridge tournaments (canasta was still unknown) also left their children in hired hands. To make matters worse, the magistrate added, the typist would expose herself to temptations. The magistrate seemed to believe that an office (the boss, male employees at all levels) was a cauldron of dangers for a woman determined to earn her own living. He was obsessed by that image.

As I insisted on defending the rights of women to work and to live on an equal footing with men, he concluded by saying: "But, Madam, remember your parents, the way they have educated you. What have you seen in your own family? Was your father the head or not? What role did your mother have?" I responded that although I loved my parents very much, I had never shared their ideas on that point, nor even on others, which of course was neither original nor exceptional. The generations that succeed each other rarely agree with one another. Especially these days. The magistrate heard me as one hears the rain.

We went from that subject to the subject of children born out of wedlock and those born of adultery. It is obvious that I found it absurd that those recently come to our vale of tears would be condemned to expiate for the sins—if they were sins—of their fathers. Naively—according to the judge— I thought that all children were natural and that only the parents could be accused of being unnatural. This assertion infuriated the magistrate.

He responded that if a man were tempted beyond his strength he shouldn't be exposed to the possibility of falling into the trap of some adventuress who might break up his home. What wouldn't a woman without scruples do to get money from him if the law didn't intervene? If children were all equal before the law, the tranquillity of the home would be forever compromised, threatened, and destroyed. I asked him then if there wasn't some advantage in that men might learn to resist temptations and to realize the kinds of situations to which these temptations might expose them. The magistrate smiled at me with paternal indulgence. "Men, Madam, are often weak when confronted by temptation. The law must take this into account and protect them." The reply came by itself. "And women?" No. Women, if they were respectable, knew how to avoid those temptations that for men were not resistible (and for that reason itself were excusable). If the law gave them the chance, the adventuresses, experts in masculine weakness, would take even more advantage of such situations than they had already.

For the magistrate in question, it was always the woman who offered the fruit of the tree of good and evil. As he talked of all this, he spoke in clipped tones. Legitimate children, born of legal marriages had to be protected. And the other kind? Their situation was to be lamented, but what could one do? There are such sad fates in life. "No," I shouted. "That is precisely the case in which sad fate does not come into play; it is rather a case of men's egotism." In response, he again asked me what I had observed in my own family.

Finally he said to me: "Madam, you are a widow, are you not? And independent, from the economic point of view?" I answered "yes" for the first time in that interview.[12] "Then," he went on "why do you bother yourself with problems that are not yours?"

Since there was talk of giving the husband the power to annul his marriage if he could prove that his wife was not a virgin, we discussed the subject of virginity with another magistrate. First I asked if the woman could annul the contract for the same reasons. With that smile of commiseration that I already knew well, the magistrate answered: "Naturally not." I asked if virginity in the widow was also required. New smile—they are a different case, he assured me. (The magistrate thought, no doubt, that he was dealing with an idiot or a shameless woman.) I asked then if he and those other gentlemen found it just as easy to pronounce judgment on similar questions. If their analysis of virginity might not be used to support deplorable abuses and every kind of blackmail. I asked if that clause about causes for annulment was not humiliating and intolerable from the woman's point of view. The magistrate did not show that he had very clear ideas on the point.

In England it is not until 1916 that Asquith stops opposing the political rights of women. And only in 1919 do they remove the barriers to entry into the professions. The same year the first woman, Lady Astor, sits in the British House of Commons. Even today, 1954, women are not admitted in the House of Lords. In that respect, what John Stuart Mill wrote in his *The Subjection of Women* continues to be true: "But Queen Elizabeth or Queen Victoria, had they not inherited the throne, could not have been entrusted with the smallest of the political duties, of which the former showed herself equal to the greatest."[13]

A Room of One's Own appears in 1929, *Three Guineas* in 1938. As impossible as it may seem today, the struggle for women's rights was not completed, even though, thanks to World War I, the movement had gained decisively. Virginia writes in her diary, on the eve of launching *A Room of One's Own*: "I am afraid it will not be taken seriously. Mrs. Woolf is so accomplished a writer that all she says makes easy reading. . . . "[14] But she has written that book with passion and conviction. What she longs for are not praises for her skill as a writer. And as for *Three Guineas,* page after page have sprung from her pen, she tells us, "like a physical volcano."[15]

In the years between the Victorian era and ours, how many forms of reactions have there been against the patriarchal dictatorship, against that male right to treat "respectable" women as obedient nurses and chained virgins, and to treat the other women, those who aren't "respectable," as vile cattle. We only have to look around to find the answer.

If we could study the intimate life, the infancy, the adolescence of famous women—those who for one reason or another have excelled in the last hundred years—we would discover the preponderant role played in those lives by the rebellion against feeling themselves the eternal nurse, the eternal virgin, the eternal flock of sheep. We would realize then the humiliation of enduring the arbitrary masculine dictatorship, whether it came from the most affectionate of fathers or from the most altruistic brother. For if our century is that of recognizing the rights of the proletariat, it is also, with greater reason, the century of the emancipation of women. (The "feminine proletariat" embraces all classes, equally suppressed by male tyranny, while the "proletariat" only applies to one class.) That is to say that this is the century in which women begin to be treated equally, as people and not as objects, however sacred that object might be. And it matters little that men placed "the object" on an altar, a place that made vigilance all the easier. (E-33)

Woman and Her Expression

This is an edited version of a transatlantic radio broadcast that Victoria made
to an audience in Spain and Argentina in August of 1936.[16]

Last year, by chance, I happened to overhear the telephone conversation of a businessman calling Buenos Aires from Berlin. He was talking to
his wife, giving her an assignment. He began this way: "Don't interrupt me."
She obeyed so perfectly, and he took his monologue so seriously, that the reg-
ulation three minutes went by without the poor woman having the chance
to utter a sound. And as my businessman was parsimonious, the conversation ended there. I, who have been invited to come talk to you and who
am being paid to do it, would like to say to you: "Interrupt me. This business of the monologue doesn't make me happy. It is to you, and not to myself, that I want to speak. I want to feel your presence. And how can I know
that you are present, that you are listening to me, if you don't interrupt me?"

I am afraid that this feeling is very feminine. If the monologue is not
enough to make women happy, it seems to have been sufficient to men's
happiness for years and years. I believe that for centuries all conversation between men and women, as soon as it enters a certain terrain, begins with a
"Don't interrupt me" from the man. Until now the monologue seems to
have been the preferred means of expression adopted by men. (Conversation
among men is nothing more than a dialogue form of this monologue.)

You could say that a man does not feel, or feels only slightly, the need
for interchange in conversation with that other being who is similar and
yet different from him: woman. In the best of cases, he has no fondness
for interruptions. In the worst case, he forbids them. Hence, man is content
to talk with himself and little does it matter to him whether the woman
hears him or not. As for him listening to a woman, it scarcely occurs to him.

For centuries, having fully realized that the argument of the strongest is
always the best argument (however much this ought not to be so), women
have resigned themselves, for the most part, to repeating little crumbs of
male monologue, at times interspersing something of their own between
these crumbs. For a woman, this whole performance of behaving like a faithful dog seeking refuge at the feet of the master who punishes her has proven
tiresome and useless.

Struggling against these qualities that man has often interpreted as signs
of a nature inferior to his own, or that he has respected because they helped
to transform woman into a statue to be placed in its niche so that it stayed

there *sage comme une image;* struggling, I say, against that tendency that leads her to offer herself as a sacrifice, women have dared to speak out with a kind of courage unknown until now: The monologue of men neither lightens my burden nor comforts my thoughts. Why should I resign myself to repeating it? I have other things to express. Other feelings, other sorrows have shattered my life, other joys have brightened it through the centuries.

Women, according to their environment, their talent, their calling, in many fields and in many centuries—and even in those that were most hostile to women—have been trying, and each time trying harder, to express themselves. And each time they are meeting with greater success. One cannot contemplate contemporary French science without referring to Marie Curie; nor can one think about English literature without bringing up the name of Virginia Woolf, or about Latin American letters without mentioning Gabriela Mistral. As for you in Spain, to mention only one person, we envy you María de Maeztu, an admirable woman who, thanks to her authentic genius as an educator, has accomplished for young Spanish women things I would like to see done for our young Argentine women.

I am totally convinced that women are also expressing themselves beyond the realm of science and the arts and that they have already expressed themselves marvelously in these fields. I am also convinced that this expression has enriched human existence through all of time and that it has been as important in the history of humanity as the expression of men, although it is of a hidden quality, subtle and less flamboyant than man's, in the way that the plumage of the hen pheasant is less flamboyant than that of her mate.

The most complete expression of woman, the child, is a work that demands, in those who are conscious of it, infinitely more care, scrupulousness, sustained attention, delicate righting of wrongs, intelligent respect, and pure love than the work that goes into the creation of an immortal poem. This is because it not only involves carrying the child for nine months and giving birth to a being who is sound of body, but it also implies giving birth to him spiritually. That is to say, not only living beside her children and with them, but before them. I believe, above all, in the power of example. There is no other way to persuade either adults or children. There is no other way to convince them. If that fails, there is no other solution.

The essential importance of early infancy is one of the points on which modern science has recently insisted the most. It is at this precise moment in his life when the child is exclusively in the hands of the woman. It is the woman, then, who leaves her indelible and decisive mark on this still soft clay; it is she who, consciously or unconsciously, shapes it. How absurd and comical it seems, then, that men still resist the idea that women are as responsible as men. Look at the implied contradiction: that for centuries, no doubt through ignorance, the greatest responsibility of all, molding the child, has been borne by beings men consider irresponsible.

The principal difference between great artists and great saints is that artists strive to put perfection into a work that is outside themselves, while saints endeavor to put it into a work that is inside themselves, and that consequently cannot be separated from their lives.

It is conceivable that the child has often transformed woman into an artist tempted by sainthood. Because in order to strive to put perfection in that work that is hers, the child, she needs to begin by trying to put perfection into her own self and not outside herself. She needs to take the path of saints and not the one of artists. The child is not tolerant of our trying to impose perfections on him that he does not see in us.

God keep me from demeaning artists, whatever might be their defects; their past, present, or future vices; whatever might be their weaknesses. They have been, are, and will be, as necessary to us as heroes or saints. Their way is also the way of heroism and sainthood. Even when the beauty of their work, as often happens, is a compensatory beauty (that is, condemned to be realized outside themselves, because it can not be realized within themselves), it is profoundly necessary to humanity. Whatever may have been their personal miseries, what we owe to great artists is some of the best of our inheritance. Take away the contributions of Dante, Cervantes, Shakespeare, Bach, Leonardo da Vinci, Goya, Debussy, Poe, Proust—just to mention the first names that occur to me—and how impoverished we would feel! That some of these men personally may have been poor wretches who could be reproached for such and such a defect—what does it matter? They have bequeathed to us their extraordinary talents. Perhaps they knew no other happiness than suffering for their work. Their work was for them the only way of fitting into an orderly sense of the world.

This means of fulfillment is one of the things that men have denied to women. For there are certain women, just as there are certain men, who can know no other happiness than suffering to create a work of art. One of these women, who is one of the most gifted beings I know, a celebrated novelist who writes with a wondrous style, said to me: "I am not truly happy except when I am alone, with a book or paper and pen. Beside this world—so real to me—the other one vanishes." However, this woman, born into an intellectual atmosphere and with a vocation that, right from the beginning, was absolutely clear, went through some atrocious years of torment and doubts when she was young. Everything conspired to prove to her that her sex was a terrible handicap in a career of letters. Everything conspired to magnify for her what she had inherited, what all we women inherit, an inferiority complex.

We need to struggle against that complex, since it would be absurd not to comprehend its importance. The spiritual state it inevitably creates is one of the most dangerous. And I see no other way of struggling against it than by giving women as solid, as carefully conceived an education as men, and to respect woman's freedom exactly as we respect the freedom of men. Not only in theory, but in practice. In theory, most civilized countries accept this idea. Unfortunately, Argentina has not advanced that far. Among our people, women have not attained, either in theory or in practice, the position they ought to have attained. Men keep on saying to them: "Don't interrupt me." And when women assert their rights to freedom, men, judging no doubt by themselves and putting themselves in the woman's place, interpret this as "licentiousness."

Women interpret freedom quite differently. We understand that with freedom comes absolute responsibility for our actions and self-realization, with no holds barred. But this does not imply licentiousness. As for self-realization, it is intimately linked to expression, whatever form that may take. One does not express oneself except by understanding perfectly what one wants to express; or, rather, the need for expression always derives from that understanding. The understanding most important to every human being is the one that concerns the problem of his or her self-realization.

That one woman realizes herself by caring for the sick, one by teaching people how to read and write, another by working in a laboratory or writing a first-rate novel, it matters little: there are many different ways to find self-realization, and the most modest ones, just as the most eminent examples, have their own meaning and value. Personally, what interests me most is written expression, and I believe that it is here that women have a field for conquest and a harvest in the making.

It is easy to demonstrate that until now women have spoken very little about themselves directly. Men have talked at great length about women, but inevitably as a way to talk about themselves by commenting on the gratitude or disillusionment, enthusiasm or bitterness that some angel or demon left in his heart, in his flesh, in his spirit. Until now we have listened principally to men as witnesses about women. Women as their own witnesses have hardly said a word because their testimony has been considered biased and therefore suspect. It is now women's turn, not merely to talk about this unknown territory that they represent but also to speak out about men. If women achieve this, world literature will be incalculably enriched, and I have no doubt that they will do it.

I know from my own experience how poorly prepared women, and particularly South American women, are to achieve this victory. They have neither the necessary education, nor the freedom, nor the tradition. And I wonder what kind of genius could do without these three things at the same time and still produce valuable work. The miracle of a work of art is only produced when it has been quietly incubating over a long period of time.

I believe that our generation and the one that follows it, and the one yet to be born, are destined not to see this miracle but rather to prepare for it and to make it imminent. I believe that our work will be discouraging and remain largely unknown. I believe that we should resign ourselves to that situation with a sense of humility, but with deep faith in the greatness and productivity of our efforts. Our small individual lives will count for little, but all our lives together will leave such an impression on history that they will change its course. We should think about that continually so that we don't become disheartened by personal setbacks or lose sight of the importance of our mission. Our sacrifices pay in advance for what will only flower after many years, perhaps centuries. For even when we have unquestionably acquired the education, the freedom, and a little tradition we will not yet have achieved everything. I allude to literary tradition that scarcely exists for women; the literary tradition of men is not one that can orient us, and at times it even contributes to distortions. We will need to become mature as we attain our education and freedom and tradition. We will have to familiarize ourselves with these advances and stop looking upon them with the eyes of a parvenu.

Thus what our effort buys now is the future for women. It will not benefit any of us personally. But this need not sadden us. Instead, this maternal feeling toward all future women ought to sustain us today. We must bolster ourselves with the conviction that the quality of that future humanity depends on our humanity, and that we are responsible for it. We must not forget that what each of us achieves in her small life has immense importance, immense power when all our lives are joined together. None of our acts is insignificant and our very attitudes add to or subtract from this sum total that we all form and that will tilt the balance.

I have just said that South American women find themselves in an inferior position with respect to women who live in certain great countries. I will add that this is to some degree their own fault. Until now they have resigned themselves much too easily to their condition. Perhaps some naive women may have been afraid of displeasing men, without realizing that they will always please them, despite everything, and that men would be in serious straits if they had to do without women. It even seems quite probable to me that women will please men more when men become accustomed to seeing them as thinking human beings who are capable of standing up to them and of interrupting them if necessary; not as objects more or less cherished, more or less indispensable to their pleasure and their comfort. More or less, you might say, as warriors' playthings. If it doesn't happen this way, it will mean that we must begin to re-educate men and to realize that the education that has made them arrogant is worthless and no longer counts.

It is characteristic of our present world that what happens in one country has repercussions from one country to another, from one continent to another. And these repercussions are almost explosive, whether we like it or not. Your compatriot Salvador de Madariaga was talking a while ago about the irresistible growth of international solidarity. He calls it "subjective solidarity" when it pertains to ideas and feelings and "objective solidarity" when it concerns actions and vested interests, and he attributes the world crisis to the lag of the first behind the second.

Therefore, with events such as they are today, the lot of women in China or in Germany, in Russia or in the United States—in the end it doesn't matter in what corner of the world—implies an extremely grave consequence for us all since we will bear the repercussions of its effects. Thus the lot of South American women vitally concerns Spanish women and women in all other countries.

I would like women all over the earth to be united in a solidarity that is not only objective, but subjective. Such an aspiration may seem too ambitious, even absurd, but I cannot resign myself to anything less.

I would wish that the sum of all our efforts, of our lives, 99 percent of which remain hidden and anonymous, will tilt the balance towards the good—toward the side that will make women enriched human beings, toward the side where it will be possible for them to give complete expression to all facets of their personalities (not only their physical expression), toward the side that will make men complete human beings to whom the monologue is no longer enough and who, from interruption to accepted interruption, naturally arrive at a dialogue with women. (E-8)

CHAPTER NINE ⁓ AFTERWORD

Victoria was a complex person with many contradictions. She could be impetuous, impatient, jealous, and violent; she could be a social snob and she certainly could react in excessive ways. But she was also honest, enthusiastic, positive, energetic, generous, and persevering, with a lively curiosity and a sense of humor. She made no secret of her faults. Indeed, she fully acknowledged the enigmas in her life that she said would torment her until her final breath.

Despite her frequent displays of self-confidence, it seems likely that Victoria suffered from a basic sense of insecurity that goes back to her early rejection by the boys she played with in her childhood, to the severe criticism of her early essays, to her own misgivings about her ability as a writer, and to growing up in a society where women were treated as second-class citizens. She also bore the indirect feeling of inferiority that came from feeling that Argentina was culturally inferior to Europe. But this sense of inferiority and discontent in no way stopped Victoria; instead, it seemed to fuel her ambition. For undoubtedly her longing to be taken seriously as an intellectual and to have Argentina regarded as a cultural center of international renown helped to prepare the ground for the founding of *Sur,* an event which Borges called "one of the most significant events of Argentine culture."[1]

A serious fault of which Victoria has been accused is that, although she had a strong feminist voice in *Testimonios,* her record with *Sur* was not impressive in advancing the cause of feminism. Janet Greenberg has suggested that Victoria's tendency to defer to the men who helped run *Sur* set a tone that gave feminism a low profile and concluded that Ocampo seemed to fail in translating her own feminine perspective into the mainstream of *Sur*'s discourse.[2]

While there is certainly some basis for Greenberg's criticism, Victoria's behavior may be partially explained by the fact that, never liking confrontation, she preferred to save her feminist energy for her own books, where she could be in complete control. There were ample alternative opportunities for Ocampo to express her feminist views in the ten volumes of her *Testimonios,* in *De Francesca a Beatrice,* and in *Virginia Woolf en su diario,* and she took good advantage of them.

More basically, I believe this criticism misses the point. From the beginning, *Sur*'s stated aim was to foster international exchange—and this it did splendidly. It was never perceived by Victoria as a feminist vehicle. Taking *Sur* as a whole over the years, it is clear, however, that it did a great deal to boost the cause of women. An examination of its over 360 issues reveals that there are many works by and about women. For while *Sur* gave most of its space to male writers, it also made room for a number of women to express their ideas in essays, stories, and poetry, as well as in a number of book and film reviews. Some of the most well-known women who were contributors were writers of stature such as María Luisa Bombal, Ana María Matute, Gabriela Mistral, Sylvia Molloy, Victoria's sister Silvina Ocampo, Susan Sontag, Diana Trilling, and Virginia Woolf. They were, as Greenberg contends, relatively few and far between, but I believe that their very presence and the high quality of their writing enhanced the cause of feminism. In addition, specific women, such as Simone de Beauvoir, Mary McCarthy, Nancy Mitford, and Carmen Bravo Villasante, were highlighted in essays and book reviews, thus giving women and their views greater visibility.

An outstanding example of *Sur*'s focus on a specific woman appears in the issue for December 1951. There, *Sur* published two essays, one by Octavio Paz, the other by Fryda Schultz de Mantovani, focusing on Sor Juana de la Cruz, the seventeenth-century Mexican nun who might well be regarded as the first Latin American feminist writer. Most importantly, these essays were followed by a reprint in its entirety of Sor Juana's famous essay, her "Respuesta a Sor Filotea" (Answer to Sister Philotea), written in response to her bishop's reprimand that she was dedicating herself to profane (and often polemic), rather than sacred, letters. Sor Juana's articulate response to her antifeminist bishop, hiding behind the pseudonymous veil of "Sor Filotea," is a brilliant and learned defense of her passionate need to continually read and learn and an account of her personal struggle to find her own intellectual life. It is, as well, a rousing exhortation to women to be educated, to read, to learn, and if they are so inclined, to persevere in their search for their own intellectual lives. Daring words in the Mexico of 1691 and still provocative in the Argentina of 1951.

Sur is to be credited with introducing Virginia Woolf to a substantial audience in Latin America in the 1930s with Spanish translations of *A Room of One's Own* (in four installments) and *Three Guineas*. Noting that Virginia Woolf had a great influence on Latin American literature, John King praised "the splendid translations" of Woolf's books in *Sur* and added: "Ocampo disseminated Woolf's work in Latin America at a very early date and thus helped to place on the agenda the problems of women in general (Argentine women still did not have the vote) and women writers in particular. Ocampo could thus use 'a publishing house of her own' to help combat some of the injustices revealed by Woolf's analyses."[3]

In 1970 an entire issue of *Sur* was devoted to women. It has many interesting articles by and about women, including a message from Indira Gandhi, an essay by Golda Meir on women and peace, an article by Mildred Adams of *The New York Times* dealing with feminism in the United States (the reality behind the myth), and a reprint of the United Nations' *Declaration on the Elimination of Discrimination against Women.* In her own opening essay "La Trastienda de la Historia" (The Backroom of History), Victoria appears to be sensitive to possible criticism—subsequently made by Greenberg—that this dedicated issue came so late in her life. She confessed that she had wanted to do such an issue for many years but that it was not a "literary" topic so that the men who shared her work on the literary journal had little interest in it. Remembering Victoria's aims for *Sur* as well as her tendency to defer to men, this is not altogether surprising.

Victoria evolved her own brand of feminism, which had several strengths. First among them is that it was born of a healing vision based on love and respect, one that imagined a world where men and women would be complementary and equal. This gave her a constructive, balanced approach that allowed her to take a broad view of feminist issues. She was concerned with the intellectual development of women's lives as well as their political, social, and sexual freedom. She could address such issues as the improvement of women's education, single mothers, and abortion with an expansive interpretation of women's rights. But she was also quite capable of taking a critical look at loveless sex or allegations of sexual harassment and seeing the issues in all their complexity.

It is essential in evaluating Victoria Ocampo to realize that she was a multifaceted person with a variety of interests, not all of which intersected with feminist issues. During the Spanish Civil War and World War II she gave supportive help to refugees who fled Europe, and to French intellectuals who remained. She was active in PEN and had a long time interest in UNESCO, to which she left her two houses, Villa Ocampo and Villa Victoria, with the idea of having artists and writers use them in a continuing pattern of cultural exchange. Because she had a sense of solidarity with diverse groups, she did not always think first in terms of gender. All of this helped Ocampo to write essays that advanced the cause of feminism by reflecting a profound humanism.

NOTES

Preface

1. "Victoria Ocampo, 88, An Author and Noted Argentine Publisher," *New York Times,* Feb. 5, 1979.
2. Beatriz Sarlo, *Una modernidad periférica: Buenos Aires 1920 y 1930* (Buenos Aires: Ediciones Nueva Vision, 1988), 85.
3. Doris Meyer, "Victoria Ocampo," *Spanish American Women Writers: A Bio-bibliographical Source Book,* ed. Diane E. Martinge (New York: Greenwood Press, 1990), 373.

Chapter One

1. Sarlo, *Una modernidad periférica,* 88.
2. Where, as here, the excerpts come from consecutive pages in the autobiography, I have given a cumulative source at the end of the sequence.
3. "Grandpa Ocampo" was really Victoria's great grandfather, Manuel José de Ocampo y González, whom the children called "Tata."
4. For a psychological interpretation of Ocampo's reading, see Sylvia Molloy, *At face value: Autobiographical writing in Spanish America* (Cambridge: Cambridge University Press, 1991), 55–75.
5. Throughout their long lives, Victoria and Angélica remained close friends, as the recent collection of letters Victoria wrote to her sister demonstrates. These letters can be found in *Cartas a Angélica y otros,* ed. Eduardo Paz Leston (Buenos Aires: Sudamericana, 1997). In the spirit of primogeniture, Angélica died in 1980, one year after Victoria.
6. This is my retelling of Ocampo's infatuation with L. G. F. Her account appears in "Le vert Paradis," in *Autobiografía I.*
7. From 1906 to 1912 Ocampo wrote Bunge hundreds of letters, which Bunge later had bound in leather and eventually returned to Ocampo. Although originally written in French, Ocampo translated some of these letters into Spanish so they could be used in her autobiography. I have included excerpts from several of Ocampo's letters to Delfina, for they give a remarkable account of her adolescent years. Because the letters are dated, I have not thought

it necessary to give individual sources. They all appear in A,2:77–139. Doris
Meyer has also translated a few of Ocampo's letters to Delfina Bunge; they
appear in DM:34–38.

As a mature woman Ocampo criticized the Bunge letters, acknowledging that, though sincere, they were both somber and emotional. The
problem, she concluded, was that they were all addressed to one person and
so only one facet of herself appeared. "My letters to Delfina are a tremendous document of adolescent arrogance and rage (of which I feel ashamed),
of continuous rebellion (that I understand and would go on feeling), a mixture of perspicacity and ignorance, of pride and humility, of wisdom and
foolishness, of clear reasoning and delirium, and spelling mistakes" (A,2:51).

Chapter Two

1. As in the previous chapter, I have not given source references for Ocampo's
    letters since they are dated. They are all to be found in volume 2 of her auto-
    biography.
2. The entire letter, in Spanish, can be found in María Esther Vásquez, *Victoria
    Ocampo* (Buenos Aires: Editorial Planeta, 1991), 44–45. For an English trans-
    lation of this letter, see DM:36.
3. Fani was "given" to Ocampo by her parents at the time of her wedding and
    forever after acted as her maid, her guard, and moral arbiter. Ocampo wrote
    an affectionate portrait of her in "Fani," T,5:108–18, "Fani," DM:200–208.

Chapter Three

1. Even many years later Ocampo showed that she was still sensitive to the
    adverse criticism of her family and friends: "Many people were scandalized
    by 'Babel.' They didn't understand me. That is the most lamentable of all.
    I was saying that, from the point of view of innate gifts, equality does not
    exist. I wasn't referring to *class,* or *money,* or *the color of a person's skin,* but
    to intelligence, talent, or physical beauty" (T,9:23).
2. For a detailed discussion of Ocampo's early essays, see Doris Meyer, "The
    Early (Feminist) Essays of Victoria Ocampo," *Studies in Twentieth Century
    Literature* 20, no. 1 (Winter, 1996).
3. Ocampo first encountered the concept of the common reader in the essays
    of Montaigne. Later, in 1925, Virginia Woolf, inspired by the same source,
    chose this phrase as the title for two books of her essays.
4. This quotation is from Ortega's lecture at the Jockey Club in December

of 1916. José Ortega y Gasset, *Meditación del pueblo joven y otros ensayos sobre América* (Madrid: Alianza Editorial, 1981), 38.

5. My English translation of *Don Segundo Sombra* was published in 1995 by the University of Pittsburgh Press.

6. In his biography of Borges, Monegal told about how Victoria and Angélica Ocampo "loved to defy Argentina's conventions by standing like gentlemen, erect against the fireplace, with cigarettes in their hands." Emir Rodríguez Monegal, *Jorge Luis Borges: A Literary Biography* (New York: E. P. Dutton, 1978), 283.

7. Ocampo translated her *Tagore en las barrancas de San Isidro* in a volume she called *Tagore on the Banks of the River Plate*. It appears in *Rabindrath Tagore: A Centenary Volume* (New Delhi: Sahitya Akademi, 1961).

8. Coincidentally, Keyserling first became aware of Ocampo in the pages of Revista de Occidente (EV:14).

9. Ocampo later confessed to Keyserling that she started each morning by turning to the overseas shipping news in *La Nación*. "I know by memory the dates of arrival and sailing for all the fastest ships. I get as much of a thrill reading the names of the transatlantic liners that I imagine will bring me your news as a person might at the mention of a street where someone they love lives" (A,4:144).

10. To this revelation, Ocampo added: "When I got to know Chanel better (the following year), she told me, among other things, that she didn't like to have sexual relations with a man more than two or three times. After that it became bothersome, men became jealous, demanding, and they offered little novelty. I said, 'Do you realize that I was once very jealous of you?' She asked me, 'Who?' and then added: 'Stravinsky?' I said: 'Oh no!' And we spoke of something else" (A,4:151).

11. Ocampo herself never drank. She claimed that she was allergic to alcohol and said she was always disturbed by the effect it had on people.

12. A more detailed description of Ocampo's first meeting with Noailles is on pp. 133–135.

13. Monnier took an interest in Ocampo. A few years later, she wrote Ocampo suggesting that the next time she was in Paris they should work together on her style. Monnier also offered Ocampo these words of advice: her writing was too modest, too timid, she needed to express her own ideas more and quote from others less, and, always, she must speak in her own name. (Adrienne Monnier to Victoria Ocampo, May 23 1935, Victoria Ocampo Papers, bMS Spa 117 (530), Houghton Library, Cambridge, Mass.)

14. "Much of Frank's communism was mystic and idealist, but he had a great

personal charm, was a skilled and persuasive lecturer, and wrote with controlled passion and enthusiasm." John King, *Sur: A study of the Argentine literary journal and its role in the development of a culture, 1931–1970* (Cambridge: Cambridge University Press, 1986), 41.

15. Ketari Kushari Dyson, *In Your Blossoming Flower Garden* (New Delhi: Sahitya Akademi, 1988), 433–34.

16. There were several people in Buenos Aires who, in the beginning, had key roles in helping Ocampo to launch *Sur*. Chief among them were Eduardo Mallea and Guillermo de Torre.

17. Rodriguez Monegal, *Jorge Luis Borges*, 235.

Chapter Four

1. King, *Sur*, 202.

2. Sarlo, *Una modernidad periférica*, 88.

3. "For most Hispanic-American writers *Sur* was a temple, a house, a place for coming together, for confrontation. Why not picture its director as a pillar of the house of letters? Pillar, support or caryatid, Victoria is something more; she is the founder of a spiritual space. Because *Sur* is not only a journal or an institution; it is a tradition of the spirit." (*Sur*, 346:92).

4. Victoria Ocampo to María de Maeztu, July 1935, Victoria Ocampo Papers, bMS Spa (829), Houghton Library, Cambridge.

5. While Victoria was in prison she found herself, for the first time in her life, without books. A priest smuggled in a Bible for her and she asked for, and received, the works of St. Theresa of Ávila, St. Augustine and the poems of St. John of the Cross. During her long dark nights in prison, Victoria meditated on Gandhi, "the contemporary whom I most venerated and whose existence . . . was for me a lesson, a presence and a balm. By his example he proved to me the exactness of an aphorism from the *Upanishads*: 'A man becomes what he thinks.'" (E-12:12)

6. The collection of Ocampo's letters in the Houghton Library at Harvard University reveals that she regularly wrote to a staggering number of people, including Virginia Woolf, Gabriela Mistral, Anita Loos, and Thomas Merton.

7. Another account of Ocampo's first encounter with Virginia Woolf is given in the vignette on pp. 135–36.

8. Virginia Woolf to Victoria Ocampo, December 22, 1934, Victoria Ocampo Papers, bMS Spa 117 (785), Houghton Library, Cambridge.

9. Virginia Woolf to Victoria Ocampo, January 22, 1935, Victoria Ocampo Papers, bMS Spa 117 (785), Houghton Library, Cambridge.

10. Virginia Woolf to Victoria Ocampo, February 26, 1935, Victoria Ocampo Papers, bMS Spa 117 (785), Houghton Library, Cambridge.

11. Victoria Ocampo to Virginia Woolf, Este miércoles, 1934 Victoria Ocampo Papers, bMS Spa 117 (841), Houghton Library, Cambridge.

12. It was in the summer of 1939 that Victoria brought the photographer Gisèle Freund to Woolf's house in Tavistock Square where Woolf sat for the now famous series of photographs of her.

13. Doris Meyer, "The Correspondence of Gabriela Mistral and Victoria Ocampo: Reflections on American Identity," *Journal of the Institute of Romance Studies* 4 (1996), 272.

Chapter Five

1. As the young author of *Sab* (1841) and *Dos Mujeres* (*Two Women,* 1842), Avellaneda was famous in Cuba and Spain as a woman with a scandalous private life and as the promoter of radical, feminist ideas. See the article in *Reinterpreting the Spanish American Essay: Women Writers of the Nineteenth and Twentieth Centuries,* ed. Doris Meyer (Austin: University of Texas Press, 1995), in which Nina M. Scott, the translator of *Sab,* assesses Avellaneda's provocative essay "La Mujer" (The Women). The essay is translated in the companion volume, *Rereading the Spanish American Essay,* ed. Doris Meyer (Austin: University of Texas Press, 1995).

2. See the article about Storni by Gwen Kirkpatrick, in Meyer, *Reinterpreting the Spanish American Essay.* For my translation of several of Storni's essays, see Meyer, *Rereading the Spanish American Essay.*

Chapter Six

1. *Sur,* 32:67–74.

2. *Virginia Woolf en su diaro* (Virginia Woolf in Her Diary) (Buenos Aires: 1954). Ocampo was reading Gide's journal, perhaps as a result of seeing it mentioned in Woolf's diary entry for August 30, 1934. Woolf commented that Gide's journal was "full of startling recollections—things I could have said myself." *A Writer's Diary: Being Extracts from the Diary of Virginia Woolf,* ed. by Leonard Woolf, New York: Harcourt Brace Jovanovich, Inc., 1973, 215.

3. In a letter to Angélica written in Paris on Feb. 26, 1975, Victoria mentioned that she had just met Susan Sontag. She added: "We understand each other very well. She had asked Cozarinsky (an Argentine writer and film maker) to introduce her to me because she said she had wanted to know

me for years. What a miracle!" Victoria Ocampo, *Cartas a Angélica y otros,* ed. Eduardo Paz Leston (Buenos Aires: Sudamericana, 1997), 210.

Chapter Seven

1. Putting Tagore in the company of Gandhi and Nehru when it came to women may seem strange after the way we saw Tagore assume the role of guru/master to Victoria's student/servant/muse in Chapter 3. Victoria was taking a generous view of Tagore here, a view that is discussed in some detail by Doris Meyer on page 70 of her biography of Ocampo.
2. *The Book of Abigail and John,* ed. L. H. Butterfield, M. Friedlander, and M. Kline (Cambridge: Harvard University Press, 1975), 120–23, 127.

Chapter Eight

1. Elizabeth Gaskell, *The Life of Charlotte Brontë* (Middlesex, England: Penquin, 1975).
2. Ibid., 172.
3. Ibid., 173.
4. Ibid., 285–86.
5. Virginia Woolf, *The Common Reader* (New York: Harcourt Brace and World, 1953), 165.
6. Emily Brontë, *Wuthering Heights and Poems* (London: J. M. Dent, 1993), 304.
7. Ibid., 360.
8. Virginia Woolf, *A Writer's Diary* (New York: Harcourt Brace Jovanovich, 1973), 5.
9. Virginia Woolf, *Three Guineas* (New York: Harcourt Brace Jovanovich, 1966), 38.
10. "The Distracting Derby," *Pall Mall Gazette,* June 5, 1913.
11. Ibid., June 6–15, 1913.
12. Ocampo's husband, Monaco Estrada, died in 1933.
13. John Stuart Mill, *The Subjection of Women* (Buffalo: Prometheus Books, 1986), 59.
14. *A Writer's Diary,* 145.
15. Ibid., 276.
16. My translation of this essay, "La mujer y su expresión," appears in its entirety in Meyer, *Rereading the Spanish American Essay,* 126–34.

Afterword

1. Victoria Ocampo, *Diálogo con Borges,* Buenos Aires: 1967, 78.

2. Janet B. Greenberg, "The Divided Self: Forms of Autobiography in the Writings of Victoria Ocampo" (Ph.D. diss., University of California, Berkeley, 1986), 311–20.

3. For an English translation of Sor Juana's "Respuesta a Sor Filotea." See: Juana Inés de la Cruz, *The Answer/ La Respuesta.* Trans. and ed. by Electa Arenal and Amanda Powell. New York: The Feminist Press at the City University of New York, 1994. A bilingual presentation of Sor Juana's important play *El Divino Narciso* can be found in Sor Juana Inés de la Cruz *The Divine Narcissus/ El Divino Narciso,* translated and annotated by Patricia A. Peters and Renée Domeier, O.S.B., Albuquerque, University of New Mexico Press, 1998.

4. King, *Sur,* 77, 80–81.

Selected Bibliography

Primary Sources

BOOKS BY VICTORIA OCAMPO (LISTED CHRONOLOGICALLY)

De Francesca a Beatrice. Madrid: Revista de Occidente, 1924.

Testimonios I. Madrid: Revista de Occidente, 1935.

Domingos en Hyde Park. Buenos Aires: SUR 1936.

Testimonios II. Buenos Aires: SUR, 1941.

Testimonios III. Buenos Aires: Editorial Sudamericana, 1946.

Soledad Sonora [*Testimonios* IV]. Buenos Aires: Editorial Sudamericana, 1950.

El viajero y una de sus sombras: Keyserling en mis memorias. Buenos Aires: Editorial Sudamericana, 1951.

Virginia Woolf en su diario. Buenos Aires: SUR, 1954.

Testimonios V. Buenos Aires: SUR, 1957.

Tagore en las barrancas de San Isidro. Buenos Aires: SUR, 1961.

Testimonios VI. Buenos Aires: SUR, 1963.

Testimonios VII. Buenos Aires: SUR, 1967.

Diálogo con Borges, Buenos Aires: SUR, 1969.

Testimonios VIII. Buenos Aires: SUR, 1971.

Testimonios IX. Buenos Aires: SUR, 1975.

Testimonios X. Buenos Aires: SUR, 1977.

Autobiografía Vol. I: El archipiélago. Buenos Aires: Ediciones Revista *Sur,* 1979.

Autobiografía Vol. II: El imperio insular. Buenos Aires: Ediciones Revista *Sur,* 1982.

Autobiografía Vol. III: La rama de Salzburgo. Buenos Aires: Ediciones Revista *Sur,* 1982.

Autobiografía Vol. IV: Viraje. Buenos Aires: Ediciones Revista *Sur,* 1982.

Autobiografía Vol. V: Figuras simbólicas—Medida de Francia. Buenos Aires: Ediciones Revista *Sur,* 1983.

Autobiografía Vol. VI: Sur y Cía. Buenos Aires: Ediciones Revista *Sur,* 1984.

CORRESPONDENCE

"Victoria Ocampo, Correspondencia," *Sur* 347 (Buenos Aires,1980).
Victoria Ocampo Papers, bMS Spa 117, Houghton Library, Harvard
   University, Cambridge, Mass.
Cartas a Angélica y otros, edited by Eduardo Paz Leston. Buenos Aires:
   Sudamericana, 1997.

Secondary Sources

BOOKS

Greenberg, Janet B. "The Divided Self: Forms of Autobiography in the
   Writings of Victoria Ocampo." Ph.D. diss., University of California,
   Berkeley, 1986.
King, John. *Sur: A study of the Argentine literary journal and its role in the
   development of a culture, 1931–1970.* Cambridge: Cambridge University
   Press, 1986.
Matamoro, Blas. *Genio y Figura de Victoria Ocampo.* Buenos Aires: Editorial
   Universitaria de Buenos Aires, 1986.
Meyer, Doris. *Victoria Ocampo: Against the Wind and the Tide.* New York:
   George Braziller, 1979.
Rodríguez Monegal, Emir. *Jorge Luis Borges: A Literary Biography.* New York:
   Dutton, 1978.
Vásquez, María Esther. *Victoria Ocampo.* Buenos Aires: Editorial Planeta, 1993.

ESSAYS

Cura, María Renée. "India in Victoria Ocampo: Gandhi-Tagore-Nehru-
   Indira." In *Victoria Ocampo: An Exercise in Indo-Argentine Relationship.*
   Delhi: B. R. Publishing Corp., 1992.
Guinazu, María Cristina Arambel. "'Babel' and 'De Francesca a Beatrice':
   Two Founding Essays by Victoria Ocampo." In *Reinterpreting the
   Spanish American Essay: Women Writers of the 19th and 20th Centuries,*
   edited by Doris Meyer. Austin: University of Texas Press, 1995.
Homenaje, Victoria Ocampo, 1890–1979." *Sur* 346 (Buenos Aires, 1980).
Meyer, Doris. "Letters and Lines of Correspondence in the Essays of
   Victoria Ocampo." *InterAmerican Review of Bibliography XVII* (1992).

————. "Victoria Ocampo and Spiritual Energy." In *A Dream of Light and Shadow: Portraits of Latin American Women Writers,* edited by Marjorie Agosin. Albuquerque: University of New Mexico Press, 1995.

————. "The Early (Feminist) Essays of Victoria Ocampo." *Studies in Twentieth Century Literature* 20, no. 1 (Winter 1996).

————. "The Correspondence of Gabriela Mistral and Victoria Ocampo: Reflections on American Identity." *Journal of the Institute of Romance Studies* 4 (1996).

Molloy, Sylvia. "The theatrics of reading: body and book in Victoria Ocampo." In *At face value: Autobiographical writing in Spanish America.* New York: Cambridge University Press, 1991.

Pratt, Mary Louise. "Don't Interrupt Me: The Gender Essay and Conversation and Countercanon." In *Reinterpreting the Spanish American Essay: Women Writers of the Nineteenth and Twentieth Centuries,* edited by Doris Meyer. Austin: University of Texas Press, 1995.

Sarlo, Beatriz. "Decir y no decir: Erotismo y represión." In *Una modernidad periférica: Buenos Aires 1920 y 1930.* Buenos Aires: Ediciones Nueva Vision, 1988.

Select List of Previously Published English Translations of Ocampo's Essays

E-1   "Babel," in *Rereading the Spanish American Essay,* edited by Doris Meyer, 121–25. Austin: University of Texas Press, 1995.

E-6   "Living History," in Doris Meyer, *Victoria Ocampo: Against the Wind and the Tide,* 217–22. New York: George Braziller, 1979.

E-7   "Woman, Her Rights and Her Responsibilities," in Meyer, *Victoria Ocampo: Against the Wind and the Tide,* hereafter cited as *Victoria Ocampo:* 228–34.

E-8   "Woman and Her Expression," in Meyer, *Rereading the Spanish American Essay,* 126–34.

E-9   "Virginia Woolf in My Memory," in Meyer, *Victoria Ocampo,* 235–40.

E-10 "María de Maeztu," in Meyer, *Victoria Ocampo,* 212–16.

E-12 "Misfortunes of an Autodidact," in *Contemporary Women Authors of Latin America: New Translations,* edited by Doris Meyer and Margarite Fernández Olmos, 77–106. Brooklyn: Brooklyn College Press, 1989.

E-14 "Woman's Past and Present," in *Lives on the Line: The Testimony of Contemporary Latin American Authors* edited by Doris Meyer, 49–58. Berkeley: University of California Press, 1989.

E-19 "The Last Year of Pachacutec," in Meyer, *Victoria Ocampo,* 273–77.

E-21 "Women in the Academy," in Meyer, *Victoria Ocampo,* 278–84.

INDEX